Action English Pictures

Illustrations by
Noriko Takahashi

Text by
Maxine Frauman-Prickel

ALTA BOOK CENTER PUBLISHERS—SAN FRANCISCO

14 ADRIAN COURT, BURLINGAME, CALIFORNIA 94010 USA

Acknowledgments

We'd like to thank the ESL staff and students of Lane Community College in Eugene, Oregon, for their enthusiastic reception of this project and of Noriko's "family" of characters. Kristin Bach and Melinda Roth added extra special "action" to this book through their sequence ideas and lesson development contributions. The support and encouragement of Elizabeth Romijn and Contee Seely helped make this project a reality—from permitting us to develop picture sequences based on forty texts to letting us use the full texts from *LIVE ACTION ENGLISH* (Berkeley, Calif.: Command Performance Language Institute, 1979, 1988, 1997). The texts are as follows: *Sewing On a Button* (p.38), *Shopping for a Coat* (p.54), and *Opening a Present* (p.70).

Project Editor:	Helen Munch
Copy Editor:	Carol Ann Brimeyer
Design and Production:	Joy Dickinson/Editorial Design
Cover Design:	Bruce Marion

ALTA BOOK CENTER PUBLISHERS—SAN FRANCISCO

14 Adrian Court
Burlingame, California 94010 USA
Phone: 800 ALTA/ESL • 650.692.1285
Fax: 800 ALTA/FAX • 650.692.4654
Email: info@altaesl.com
Website: www.altaesl.com

ISBN 1-882483-71-5

Contents

To the Teacher

WELCOME to *ACTION ENGLISH PICTURES!* The picture sequences that follow are designed primarily for beginning English language learners —children and adults—from kindergarten through university, low-level or literacy classes. However, students with some literacy and familiarity with basic English sentence structure and the present, past, and future tenses can also benefit from this material.

The main purpose of *ACTION ENGLISH PICTURES* is to offer students opportunities to engage in language acquisition activities. The pictures provide the stimuli for listening and speaking, while texts created by either the teacher or students provide material for reading and writing. Complete original texts for forty of the sixty-six picture sequences in *ACTION ENGLISH PICTURES* can be found in *LIVE ACTION ENGLISH* by Elizabeth Romijn and Contee Seely (Command Performance Language Institute.: 1755 Hopkins Street, Berkeley, California 94707; 510.524.1191; consee@aol.com, 1979, 1988, 1997). The complete texts for the picture sequences found only in *ACTION ENGLISH PICTURES* are included in an appendix on pages 111-118. In addition, you will find a cross reference appendix (pages 119-120) for sequences and page numbers found in *LIVE ACTION ENGLISH.*

ACTION ENGLISH PICTURES and *LIVE ACTION ENGLISH* are based on the Total Physical Response (TPR) approach to language acquisition proposed by James J. Asher.* According to Asher, a target language can best be acquired through listening, modeling, and demonstration. With *ACTION ENGLISH PICTURES,* students first listen to English as it is modeled by the teacher, then demonstrate their understanding by responding with appropriate actions.

For example, with the picture sequence *Making Tea* (p. 15), students listen as the teacher begins, "You want some tea," then models the text and the actions, "Go to the kitchen," "Get the teapot," "Fill the pot with water," etc. After modeling the complete text and actions, the teacher asks the class (or an individual student) to demonstrate understanding by actively responding. If the students' actions don't correspond to the text, further modeling is necessary.

Beginning English language learners first introduced to English through TPR activities are ready for *ACTION ENGLISH PICTURES* as a natural extension of their language acquisition. The pictures aid students whose listening and speaking proficiencies exceed their reading ability. At the same time, the pictures provide visual contexts for "reading" exercises following the TPR lessons.

In the *Introduction* that follows, you will find some suggestions for using *ACTION ENGLISH PICTURES*. How you use the picture sequences will depend on the size of your class, the level of your students, and your imagination. We encourage you to experiment and to create your own activities to accompany the pictures. And, if you come up with any new ideas for using the pictures, let us hear from you!

Note to Teachers of Languages Other Than English

The sequences as presented in this book have proven effective for new learners of other languages as well. Since the sequence pictures are presented without written text, the teacher may add any targeted language when using the pictures in instruction. Consistent with the concept that TPR is effective for language acquisition of other languages, *LIVE ACTION ENGLISH* (the text referred to in the second paragraph) is now available in versions for teaching Spanish, French, German, Italian, and Japanese, all from Command Performance Language Institute.

Noriko Takahashi
Maxine Frauman-Prickel

*James J. Asher, *Learning Another Language Through Actions* (Los Gatos, Calif.: Sky Oaks Productions, 1977).

Introduction

The picture sequences in *ACTION ENGLISH PICTURES* are divided into seven units: *AM-PM, Health and Safety, At Home, Going Out, Holidays and Leisure, At School,* and *Weather.* The units and the sequences within the units may be presented in any order, although some teachers may prefer to present an entire unit to match a particular curriculum. The picture sequences are presented without text on reproducible tear-out pages to allow maximum flexibility in lesson planning.

UNIT ORGANIZATION

MODEL LESSONS, EXERCISE SHEETS

Each unit is introduced by a model lesson with a duplicatable exercise sheet. The purpose of the model lesson is to give you an idea of the kind of activity that can follow a particular picture sequence presentation. Additional activity suggestions accompany each model lesson. Other suggestions for extension activities appear later on in this introduction (pp. viii–x).

Each model lesson contains the text for that lesson and verb lists for the remaining picture sequences in the unit. The verb lists are intended to help you create your own texts.

PROCEDURE

THE TOTAL PHYSICAL RESPONSE APPROACH

However you choose to use *ACTION ENGLISH PICTURES*, we recommend that you begin with a Total Physical Response (TPR) lesson to familiarize students with both the context and vocabulary of each picture sequence.

The following procedure lists the steps in a TPR presentation leading to the introduction of a picture sequence. The same steps may be used with all of the sequences.

1. **Preparation.** Select a picture sequence and gather together all the props you'll need. You probably won't have enough props for everyone in the class, but you should have enough to demonstrate the actions. You might also want to choose a student helper to assist you in the demonstration.

2. **Creating the text.** Look at the pictures and decide what vocabulary (verbs and nouns) you'll need to prepare your text. (The model lesson texts and the verb lists will help you.)

3. **Presenting the vocabulary.** Isolate any new or difficult vocabulary in your text and introduce it through a mini-TPR lesson. For example, in the picture sequence *A Dental Appointment* (p. 27) you might introduce and model *waiting, press, hurt, examine, clench,* and other verbs. Use TPR and/or pictures (drawings, photos) to introduce nouns (*toothache, examining room, filling*) as well.

4. **Presenting the text.** With or without your student helper, present the text and model the actions while students listen and watch. You may want to repeat some of the actions to ensure comprehension.

5. **Repetition.** Ask the entire class to demonstrate the actions as you present the text. Look for full class participation—listening and doing, *without speaking.* The object here is for students to grasp the language by physically responding to the text. Repeat some of the text out of sequence to check comprehension and/or combine some of the commands in unexpected ways for variety. The number of repetitions will depend on the level of your class. Beginning students may want to repeat your words as they perform the actions. Such repetition is all right as long as it doesn't interfere with actual comprehension.

6. **Presenting the pictures.** Using your copy of a picture sequence, "read" through a complete sequence first while students listen. Then, ask students to repeat after you in a second "reading." Allow time for students to go over the sequence and to ask questions. Give students an opportunity to demonstrate their understanding by having them point to specific items in a picture or to a particular picture in the sequence. Distribute student copies of the picture sequence. If students can write, have them fill in the text in the spaces provided. Or make writing a separate follow-up activity in which you provide a printed text for students to copy.

7. **Practice.** Once students are able to respond to the pictures, ask them as a group to direct you, using the pictures as their guide. Then, ask for volunteers for the rest of the class to direct. Encourage the use of new text commands and combinations.

   When you feel that students are ready to work more independently, group them in pairs or in threes and fours according to ability. Give each pair or group a picture page and ask each pair or group member to direct the action of the other(s). Circulate and check for individual and common problems that might serve as the basis for follow-up lessons. Be on the lookout also for good student pairs to demonstrate in front of the rest of the class.

EXTENSION ACTIVITIES   VARIETY AND FLEXIBILITY

The following suggested activities can be used with any of the picture sequences and with beginning, intermediate, or advanced students. For our purposes, a "beginner" is a preliterate, new learner of English. An "intermediate" student has some literacy and familiarity with the simple present, continuous, and past tenses. An "advanced" student is literate, familiar with the future and present perfect tenses, and possesses sufficient vocabulary and experience to allow for in-class discussion.

Verb Forms and Tenses

Once students are familiar with the pictures and vocabulary through the TPR exercises, try having them describe the pictures in sequence using the statement form and the present continuous tense. (**Example:** "He's washing his hands," "He's drying them on a towel," etc.) Next time through, try a new tense (past or future). Ask lower level students questions such as "What's he doing?" and require an answer in the same tense: "He's *V + ing*." Have more advanced students ask other questions in a chain drill. (*Student 1 to Student 2:* "What's he doing?" *Student 2:* "He's getting the teapot.") Or isolate (or cut apart) the pictures and ask students what happened *before* and *after* each picture. Such an exercise focuses on predictive skills as well as tenses and usually calls forth imaginative responses.

Questions

Asking Yes/No and Why questions about any of the pictures can aid comprehension and question-answer formation. Have students, working in pairs or small groups, ask or write appropriate questions about individual pictures or an entire sequence. Questions can focus on vocabulary (**Example:** "What's he holding?") or speculation (**Example:** "Why does he look sad?"). Or create a game in which teams compete to correctly answer five or more questions you have written about a picture.

Describe a Picture

Select one picture in a sequence and focus on a single aspect of the scene for vocabulary development. For example, if there is a person in the picture, have students identify parts of the body, articles of clothing, and facial expression. Or select several pictures from different sequences, then describe (or have a student describe) one of the pictures and ask the rest of the class to identify it.

Tell a Story

Again using one picture, ask students to tell a story about it. If your students can write, make this a written exercise. Have students read aloud or dictate their stories while you write them down or put them on the board (as in the Language Experience Approach to reading). Tell students to title their stories and name their characters.

Cutting and Pasting

All of the sequences can be cut up, rearranged, and pasted on paper to create new sequences for picture stories. Cut up and mix the pictures of one sequence, then ask students to rearrange and number the pictures in correct order. If different pictures are used together, have students create new texts and write them under each picture. Your younger students can color the pictures.

There are many other ways in which *ACTION ENGLISH PICTURES* can be used, either in sequence or individually, with the entire class or with pairs and small groups. You will find additional activity suggestions and sample duplicatable exercise sheets at the beginning of each unit.

How to Make Transparencies

In working with *ACTION ENGLISH PICTURES*, you may want to use an overhead projector (OHP) and transparencies. (If your program doesn't have an OHP, start working on ways to squeeze one into the budget. You'll never regret it.) Projection onto a screen works best; however, if you don't have a screen, any flat light-colored wall surface will do.

One advantage of using an OHP is that the entire class can focus on the same material at the same time. Once the material is on a transparency, it can be written on, cut apart, rearranged, isolated for discussion, and many other things. Confusion, often experienced by beginning students, about what to do with a worksheet is eliminated. You can control the pace and accuracy of your students' work and reinforce learning with minimal distraction.

Making a transparency is actually quite simple. Most photocopy machines can make transparencies from originals such as the picture sequences in this book. Check the operating instructions for your particular photocopier. Usually, all you need is a sharp original to copy from and a clear plastic transparency (available from your supplier). First, load the transparency in the paper tray; then, photocopy the original onto it as you would onto a regular sheet of paper. If you don't have access to a photocopier, you can have a transparency made for about a dollar at most commercial fast photocopy outlets. (You will also probably want to buy a supply of transparency pens, available in permanent and washable ink in many colors.)

Transparencies have numerous uses. You can use them to create new stories from other graphic sources. Just cut out the parts you want, put them into some of the *ACTION ENGLISH PICTURES* sequences you have used, add characters, objects, or activities, and you have a new picture sequence. Have students, individually or in groups, write a story or text for the new sequence on a transparency. Then, project the text and ask the student(s) to read the story aloud while the rest of the class follows along. Or have students create dialogs to accompany pictures you have cut from a sequence. With one picture to guide you, help your students write short dialogs with a bus driver, a post office clerk, a receptionist in a medical office, or with any of the other characters featured.

The material you create can be used again and again. With transparencies, you won't ever have to turn your back to your students!

UNIT 1 **AM-PM**

Model Lesson

Going to Bed

Before presenting the model lesson, review the general procedure for using TPR (pp. vii–viii) to introduce the text below and the picture sequence *Going to Bed* (p. 6). When students are familiar with both the text and the pictures, distribute copies of the exercise sheet (p. 7).

LESSON TEXT   GOING TO BED (p. 6)

1. It's 10 PM. You're watching TV.
2. The program is finished.
3. You're very tired.
4. Get up and turn off the TV.
5. Stretch and yawn.
6. Go to your bedroom.
7. Turn on the lights.
8. Sit on the bed and take off your shoes and socks.
9. Stand up and get undressed.
10. Take off your sweater. Take off your pants.
11. Put on your pajamas.
12. Pull back the covers on your bed.
13. Turn off the lights.
14. Get into bed.
15. Put your head on the pillow.
16. Pull up the covers and . . .
17. Go to sleep.
18. Dream about your family.

EXERCISE   MATCHING PICTURES AND SENTENCES

Answers to Exercise:
1. You're very tired.
2. Go to your bedroom.
3. Put on your pajamas.
4. Pull up the covers.
5. Dream about your family.

Ask students to tell you about the pictures in the sequence. Then, ask them to draw lines connecting each picture to its text. If some students need assistance, have them work with other students. With more advanced students, duplicate the exercise *without* the text and ask students to write their own sentences for each picture.

ADDITIONAL ACTIVITIES   GRAMMAR, WRITING, DISCUSSION

These activities are suggested for use with the *Going to Bed* picture sequence. Many of them may be suitable for use with other sequences as well. For additional suggestions, see *Extension Activities* (pp. viii–x).

Grammar

Adverbs of frequency   Ask intermediate students about their bedtime routines and write the responses on the board (**Example:** Ling usually goes to bed at 10 PM. He never turns off the TV.). Or have students interview each other using the following worksheet format:

STUDENT A (name)	STUDENT B (name)
1. What time do you usually go to bed?	1. <u>I usually go to bed at 10 PM.</u>
2. Do you sometimes watch TV?	2. _____
3. Who usually watches TV with you?	3. _____
4. Who always turns off the TV?	4. _____
5. Who is always the first to go to bed in your family (apartment, house)?	5. _____
6. Who is always last?	6. _____
7. Do you ever remember your dreams?	7. _____
8. What do you often dream about?	8. _____

Have students write up their interviews in paragraph form using the information they have gathered, and changing the pronouns and verb forms (**Example:** *Juan/He* usually *goes* to bed at 10 PM.).

Future and past tenses   Ask high beginning and intermediate students to describe their previous night's activities and their plans for the coming evening. Begin with questions such as "Did you watch TV last night?" "How late did you watch TV?" "What did you do when you got tired?" using the past tense, and "What do you think you'll do tonight?" "How late will you stay up?" "What will you watch on TV?" using the future tense.

Two-word verbs   This sequence is rich in two-word verb expressions. Have intermediate students replace the nouns with pronouns in the following expressions:

turn off the TV (it)	turn on the lamp (it)
take off your shoes (them)	put on your pajamas (them)
pull back the covers (them)	dream about your family (them)

Writing

From the picture sequence *Going to Bed,* have beginning students choose four or five pictures that relate to their own activities. Then, have the students cut out the pictures and glue them onto another paper in sequence. Ask students to write, with your help, a sentence about themselves under each picture. When they have finished writing, ask students to exchange papers so they can read each other's stories. (Students enjoy reading their classmates' work and are able to help each other clarify the written stories.)

Discussion

The last line of the text, "Dream about your family," can be the jumping off point for some interesting discussion. Students enjoy talking about their dreams and never fail to ask for vocabulary to talk about nightmares! They may also express interest in discussing sleep-walking and sleeptalking. See if your students can describe their dreams. Ask them what they dreamed about when they knew they would be coming to this country. Did their dreams change after they arrived?

Verb Lists

GOOD MORNING (p. 8)

1. is (it's)
2. wake (up)
3. stretch
4. yawn
5. rub
6. get (up) (dressed)
7. do
8. go (to) (back)
9. wash
10. make
11. eat
12. read
13. brush
14. put (on)
15. kiss
16. leave

BREAKFAST CEREAL (p. 9)

1. eat
2. open
3. pour
4. spill
5. pick (up)
6. put
7. close
8. sprinkle (over)
9. pour (on)
10. take
11. chew
12. swallow

SCRAMBLED EGGS (p. 10)

1. fix
2. break
3. drop
4. pick (up)
5. beat
6. add
7. mix
8. oil
9. put
10. heat
11. pour
12. cook
13. stirring
14. turn (off)
15. eat

A PIECE OF TOAST (p. 11)

1. eat
2. take (out)
3. put
4. push
5. wait
6. is (it's)
7. spread
8. watch
9. melt
10. cut
11. pick (up)
12. try

A GLASS OF MILK (p. 12)

1. pour
2. spill (don't)
3. go (back)
4. pick (up)
5. get
6. wring (out)
7. wipe
8. rinse (out)
9. hang
10. is, be
11. drink

WASHING YOUR HANDS (p. 13)

1. wash
2. turn (on) (off)
3. pick (up)
4. put (down)
5. rinse
6. dry

SOUP FOR LUNCH (p. 14)

1. heat (up)
2. pick (up)
3. open
4. pour
5. add
6. stir (up)
7. put (on)
8. cover
9. turn (on) (off)
10. wait (for)
11. take (off)
12. check
13. is (it's)
14. blow (on)
15. cool (off)
16. try

MAKING TEA (p. 15)

1. want
2. go (to)
3. get
4. fill
5. put (on)
6. is (it's)
7. boil
8. put (in)
9. pour
10. drink
11. give

GETTING HOME (p. 16)

1. go
2. walk
3. take (out)
4. put
5. unlock
6. turn (on)
7. open
8. close
9. lock
10. sit (down)

Matching Pictures

Going to Bed

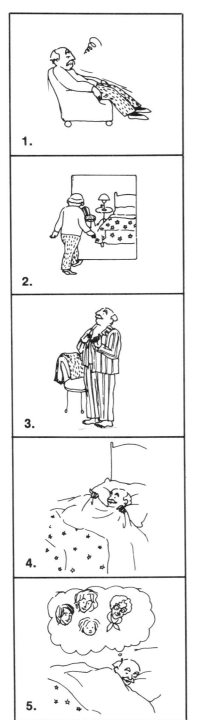

1.

2.

3.

4.

5.

Directions: Draw a line from the picture to the correct sentence below.

Put on your pajamas.

You're very tired.

Dream about your family.

Go to your bedroom.

Pull up the covers.

ACTION ENGLISH PICTURES UNIT 1 / AM-PM

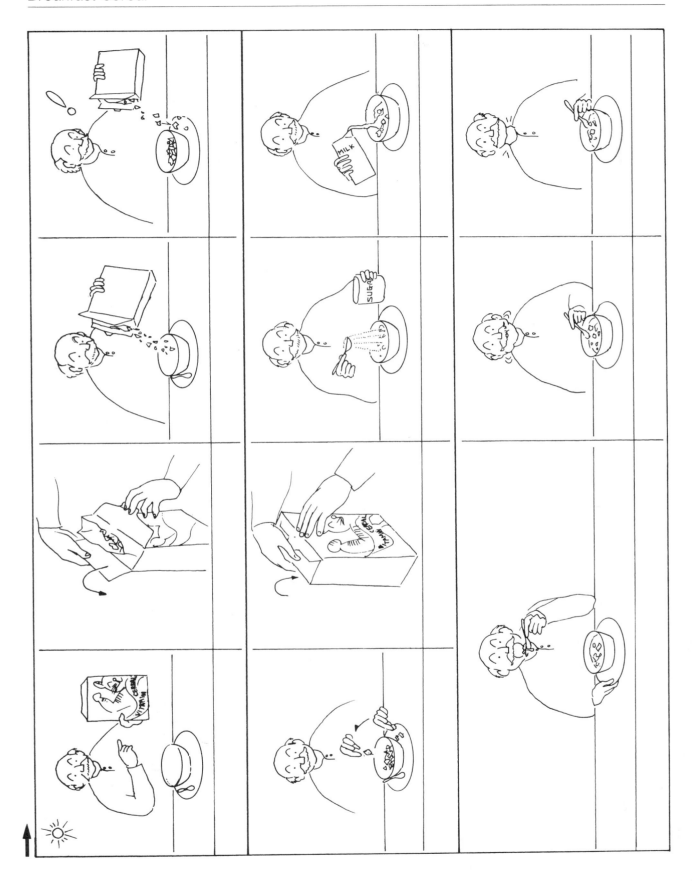

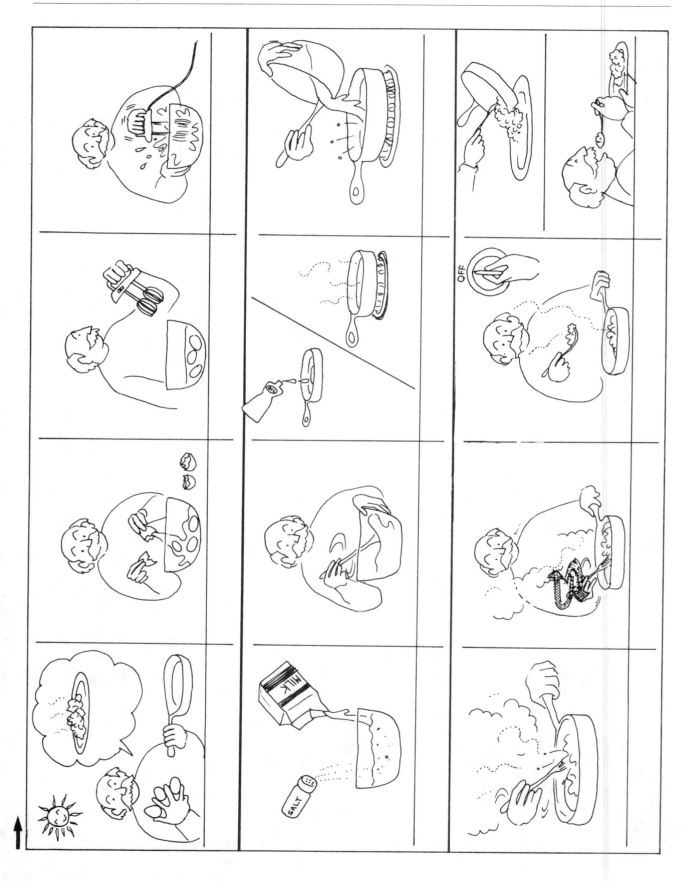

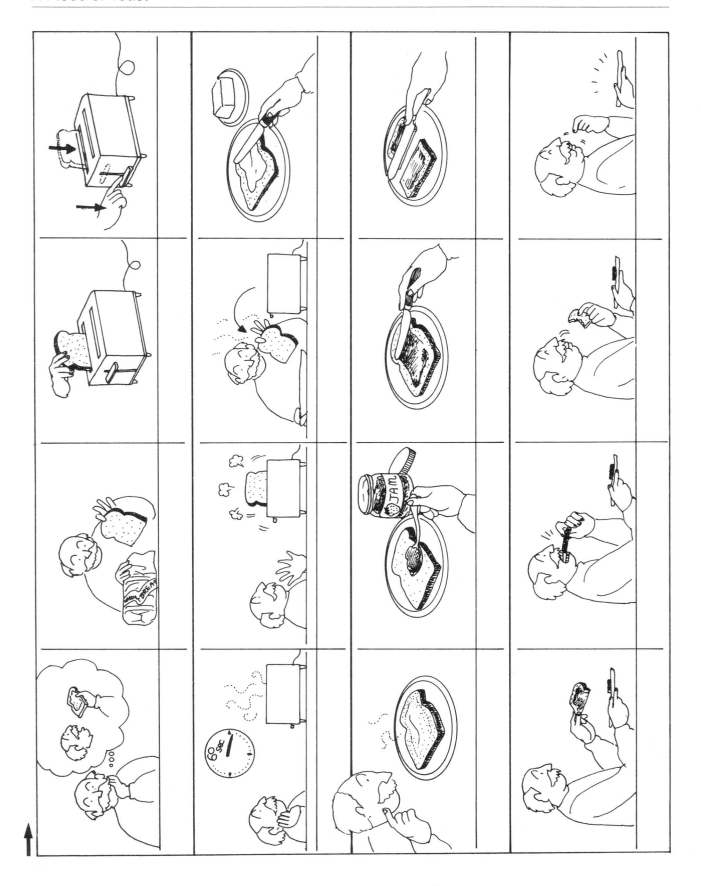

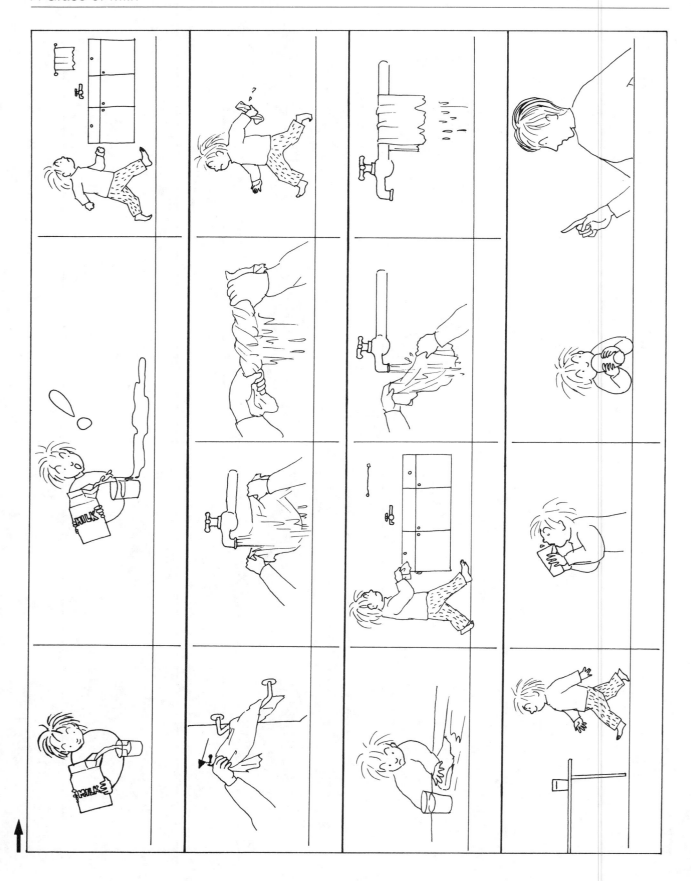

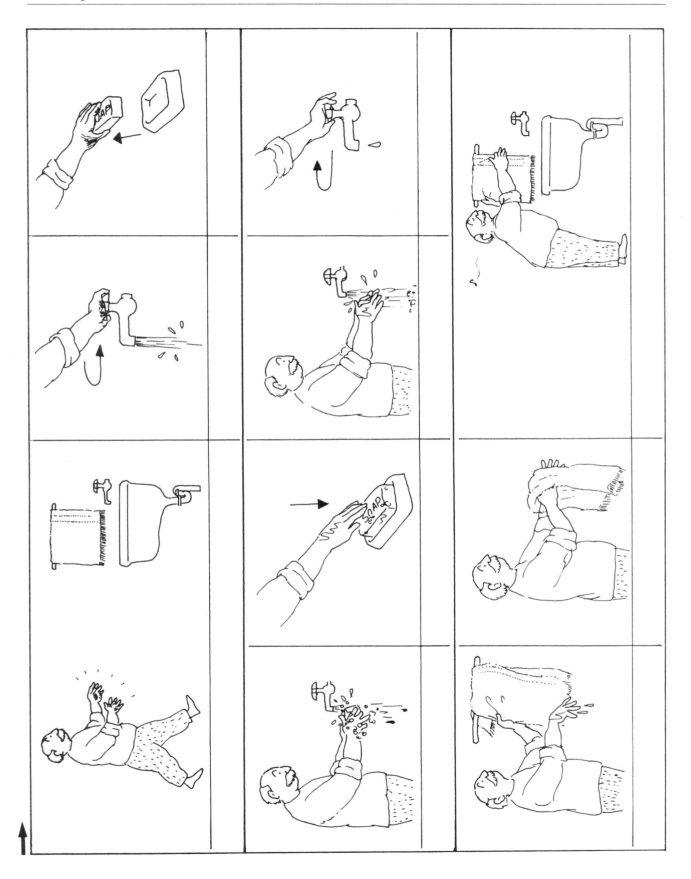

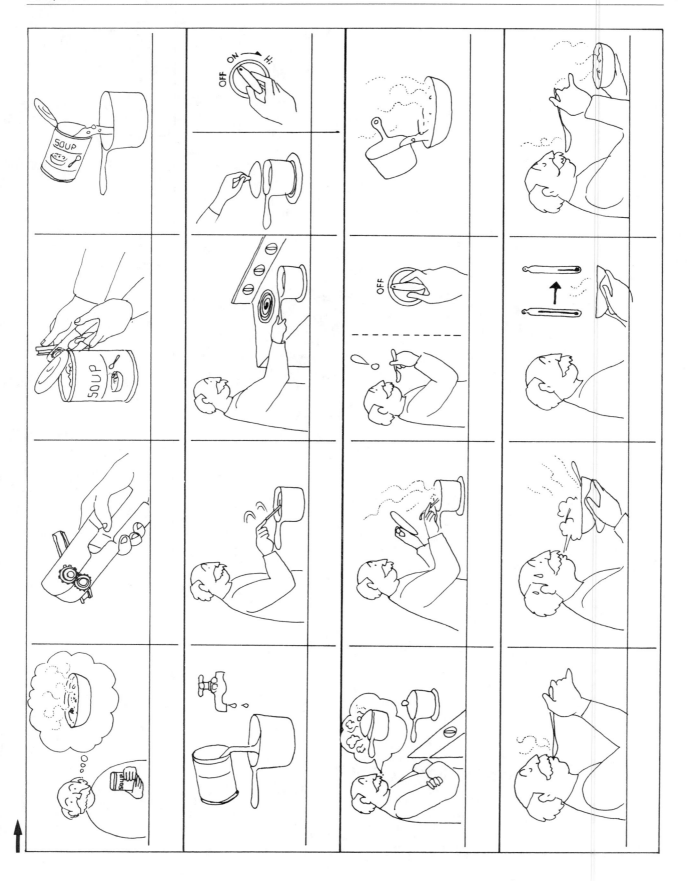

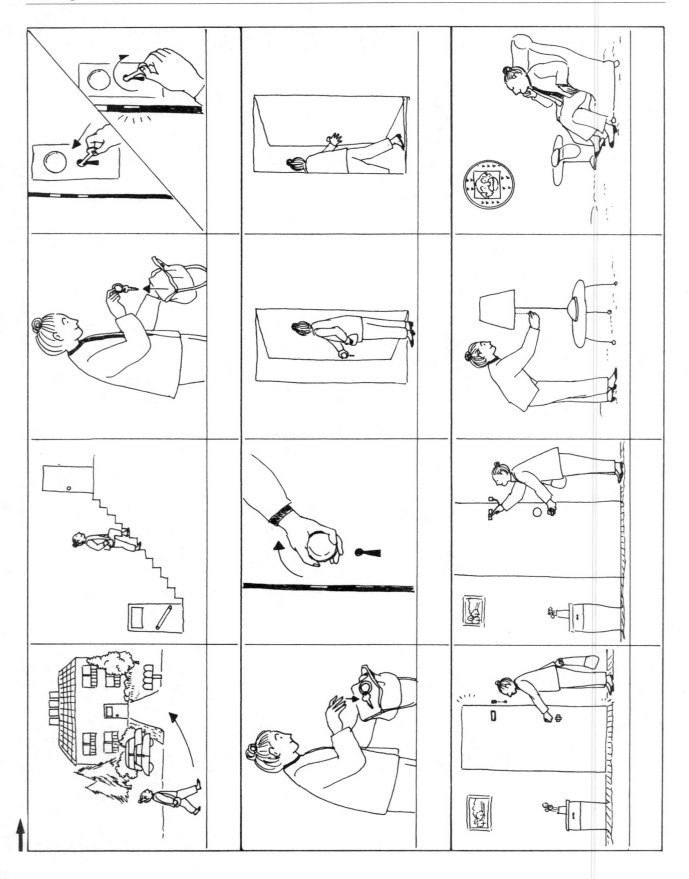

UNIT 2 **HEALTH AND SAFETY**

Model Lesson

At the Doctor's Office

Before presenting the model lesson, review the general procedure for using TPR (pp. vii–viii) to introduce the text below and the picture sequence *At the Doctor's Office* (p. 22). When students are familiar with both the text and the pictures, make class copies of the exercise sheet (p. 23).

LESSON TEXT

AT THE DOCTOR'S OFFICE (p. 22)

1. You're at the doctor's office.
2. You don't feel well.
3. The doctor comes in.
4. She shakes your hand.
5. She asks you, "What's the matter?"
6. You tell her, "I have a headache. I have a backache. I have the chills."
7. She takes your temperature.
8. She takes your pulse.
9. She listens to your heart.
10. She looks at your eyes.
11. She looks in your ears.
12. She says, "Open your mouth and say *Ahhhhhh.*"
13. She looks at your tongue and your throat.
14. She tells you, "I think you have the flu. Go home and go to bed."

EXERCISE

VOCABULARY BUILDING AND PICTURE MATCHING

Answers to Exercise:
1. The doctor looks in your ears.
2. She looks at your eyes.
3. She takes your pulse.
4. She listens to your heart.
5. She looks at your tongue.
6. She takes your temperature.
7. She looks at your throat.

This exercise can be done in a number of ways. If your students don't write easily, they can number the sentences instead of writing them. You can also create other matching exercises focusing on symptoms (backache, stomachache, chills, etc.) or a doctor-patient dialog ("Well, how are you feeling today?" "Not so good." "Open your mouth wide, please." "Ahh . . .").

ADDITIONAL ACTIVITIES

ROLEPLAYING, WRITING, DISCUSSION

These activities are suggested for use with the *At the Doctor's Office* picture sequence. Many of them may be suitable for use with other sequences as well. For additional suggestions, see *Extension Activities* (pp. viii–x).

Roleplaying

With beginning students, roleplay conversations at the doctor's office. You can take the doctor's part or select two students to roleplay.

Before beginning the roleplay, be sure your students have some basic vocabulary, such as:

ankle	leg	blister	headache	broke(n)
arm	neck	cramps	rash	sprain(ed)
back	shoulder	earache	sore	swollen
foot/feet	throat	fever	stuffy nose	twist(ed)

Keep the vocabulary list manageable to ensure better retention.

Begin the roleplay with initial questions from the doctor or nurse, such as: "What's the matter?" "What can I do for you?" "How are you today?" "What's the problem?" With intermediate students, roleplay situations involving use of the telephone for making and breaking appointments, giving information about illness, and so on. Give students a list of roleplay situations and encourage them to think up their own. If you take the part of the person receiving the call, you can keep the conversation going by asking questions such as, "How did you twist your ankle?" or "When do you think you'll be back at school?" Here are a few situations to get you started:

1. You have chills and a fever of 102°. You don't feel well enough to go to work/school. Call your boss/teacher. Tell him/her what's wrong and when you expect to be back.
2. Your child is ill. S/he has the flu and a fever. Call your child's school and tell the office clerk what the matter is.
3. You are ill and have to cancel your dental appointment. You are sneezing and coughing a lot. Call the dentist's office to cancel your appointment and make another one.
4. You twisted your ankle and can't play soccer on Sunday, but you could be timekeeper. Call your team captain and explain.
5. Your friend has been sick for a week. Call to find out how s/he is and offer your help.
6. You broke your glasses and need another pair. Call for an optometrist's appointment. Ask for directions to his/her office.
7. Your baby has a temperature of 101°. S/he is crying a lot and won't eat. Call your pediatrician and ask for advice.

Writing

Beginning students can write their own sentences if they have a model to follow. Write the following chart on the board or use an overhead projector:

I	hurt	my	eye(s)
He	look(s) at	his	ear(s)
She	listen(s) to	her	throat
The doctor	check(s)		nose
	examine(s)		mouth
	open(s)		pulse
	take(s)		temperature
			heart

Demonstrate how sentences may be formed by taking one word from each column (**Example:** "I hurt my eye." "The doctor listens to my heart."). Have students read sentences from the chart and then write down sentences that you dictate. Encourage students to write additional sentences using the chart. Add new structures to the chart:

You	doesn't/don't	feel	sick
I		has/have	a headache
He/She			a backache

Give your students a beginning sentence and have them write a story (**Example:** "When I don't feel well, I go to the doctor's office.).

Discussion

With intermediate students you can discuss and compare home remedies. Put your students in small groups and have them discuss or create remedies for these situations: a person has had too much to drink; a baby cries all the time; a child or an adult has a bad toothache.

Verb Lists

A VITAMIN PILL (p. 24)

1. take (off) (out)
2. pick (up)
3. put (back) (down)
4. drink
5. swallow
6. stuck
7. went

YOU'RE GETTING SICK (p. 25)

1. feel
2. cover
3. sneeze
4. take (out) (care)
5. blow
6. wipe
7. cough
8. leave
9. go
10. are (you're)
11. fall (down)
12. get (up)
13. buy

PUTTING DROPS IN YOUR EYES (p. 26)

1. put
2. open
3. fill
4. keep
5. hold
6. squeeze
7. blink (don't)
8. missed
9. running (down)
10. wipe (off)
11. try
12. is (that's)
13. did
14. go

A DENTAL APPOINTMENT (p. 27)

1. waiting
2. have
3. press
4. say
5. hurt
6. look (at)
7. close
8. call
9. follow
10. sit (down)
11. come (in)
12. is (what's)
13. tell
14. open
15. see (can't)
16. examine
17. clench
18. think (about)
19. fill

A BLOODY KNEE (p. 28)

1. walking
2. fall (down)
3. skin
4. scream
5. get (up)
6. cry
7. hurt
8. look (at)
9. bleeding
10. put (on) (over)
11. limp
12. buy
13. wash
14. stings
15. blow
16. unwrap
17. throw (away)

A BROKEN PLATE (p. 29)

1. broke
2. pick (up)
3. put (down) (away)
4. get
5. unscrew
6. squeeze
7. stick
8. hold
9. screw
10. dry
11. fix, fixed

A BROKEN GLASS (p. 30)

1. broke
2. pick (up)
3. be
4. cut (don't)
5. take (over)
6. throw (away)
7. get
8. go (back)
9. lean (over)
10. sweep
11. dump
12. put (away)
13. dropped, drop (don't)

FIRE! (p. 31)

1. are (you're)
2. preparing
3. playing
4. is (there's)
5. put
6. grab
7. leave
8. close
9. pick (up)
10. dial
11. tell
12. give
13. yell
14. get
15. run
16. come
17. comfort

STOP! THIEF! (p. 32)

1. rob
2. steal
3. take (out)
4. point (at)
5. say
6. stick (up)
7. grab
8. come
9. run (away)
10. stop
11. drop
12. hold (up)
13. shoot
14. pay (doesn't)

Vocabulary Building

At the Doctor's Office

Directions: Choose one of the sentences below to write under each picture.

The doctor takes your temperature.
She looks in your ears.
She takes your pulse.

She looks at your tongue.
She looks at your throat.
She listens to your heart.
She looks at your eyes.

1. _____

2. _____

3. _____

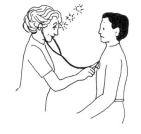

4. _____

5. _____

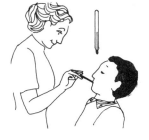

6. _____

7. _____

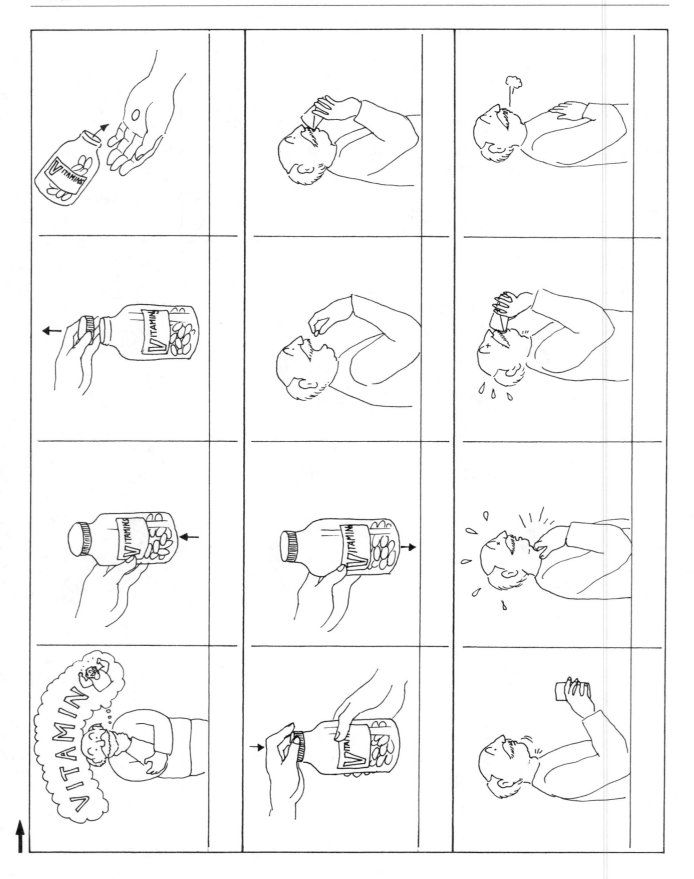

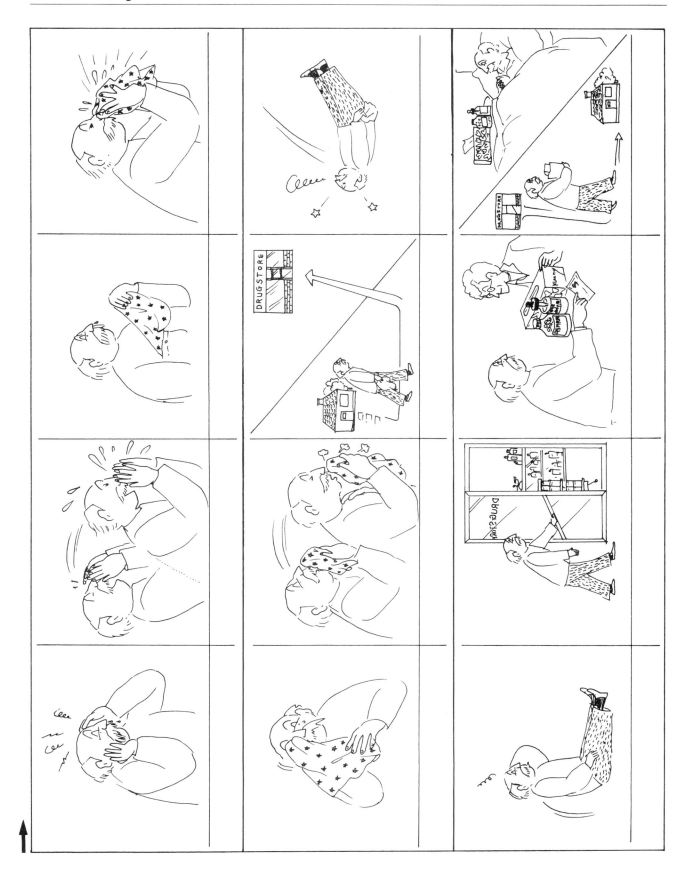

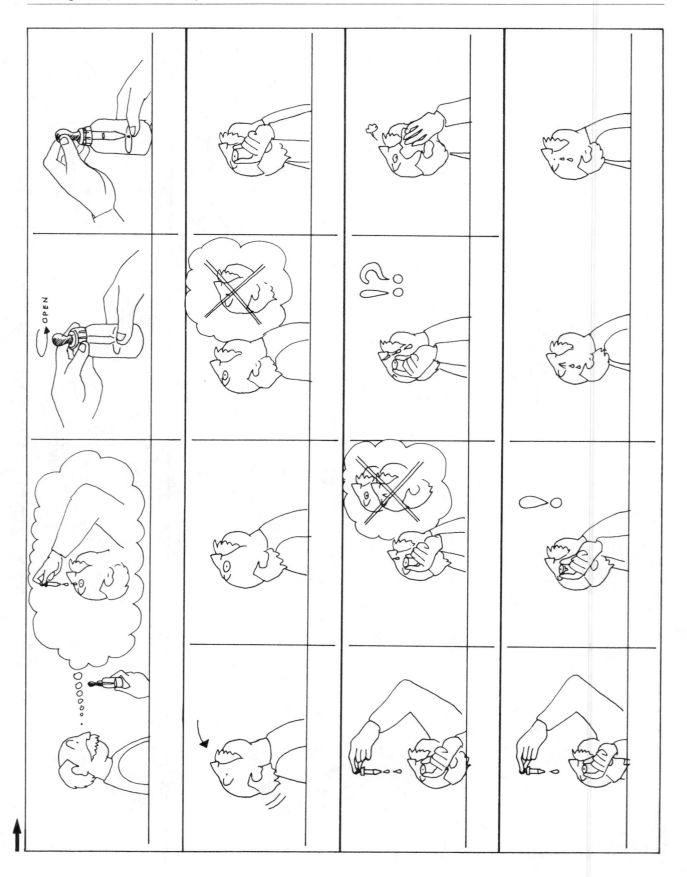

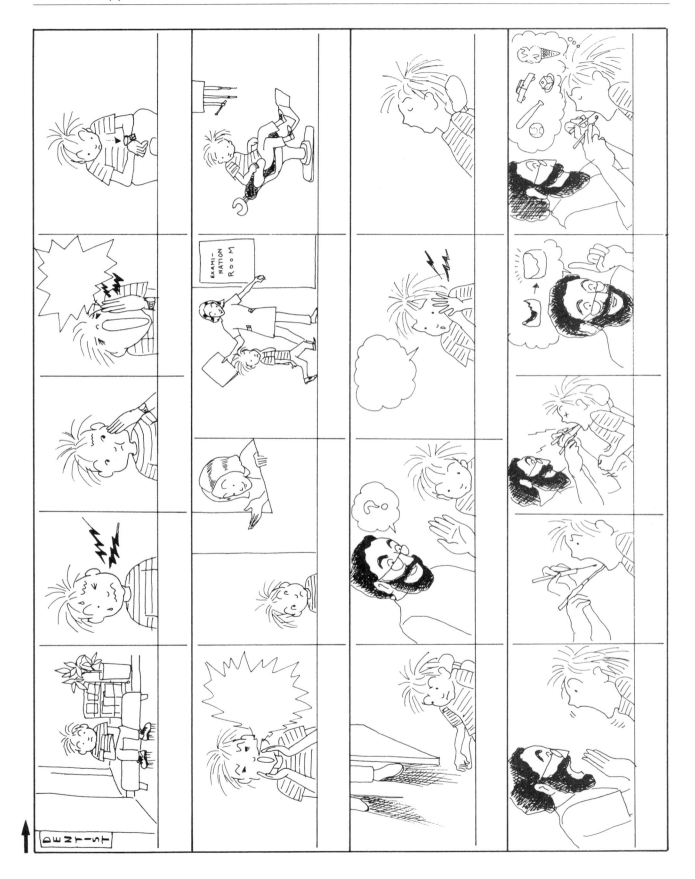

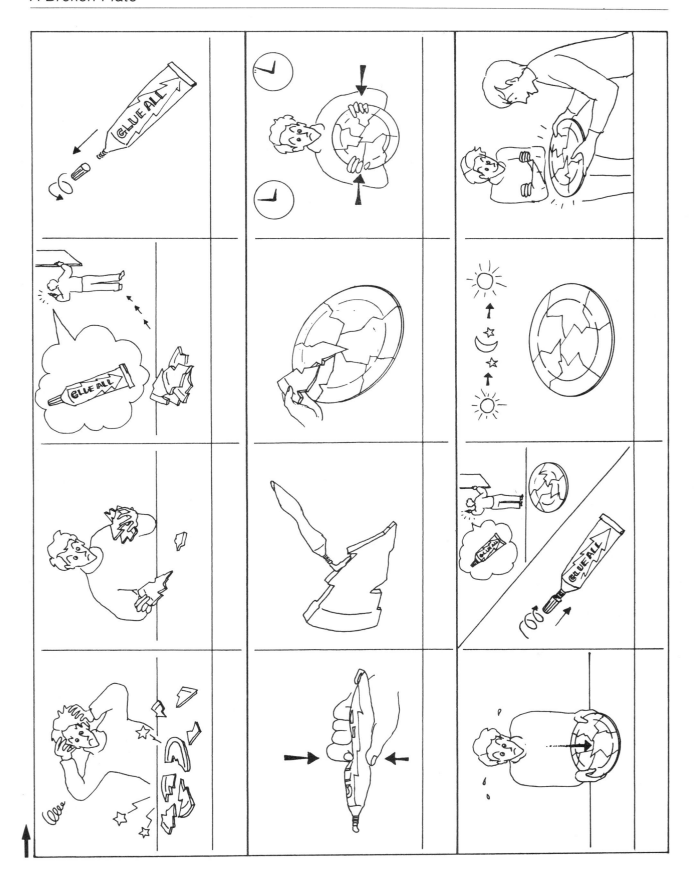

UNIT 3 **AT HOME**

Model Lesson

Sewing On a Button

Before presenting the model lesson, review the general procedure for using TPR (pp. vii–viii) to introduce the text below and the picture sequence *Sewing On a Button* (p. 38). When students are familiar with both the text and the pictures, make class copies of the exercise sheet (p. 39) and the picture sequence.

LESSON TEXT   SEWING ON A BUTTON* (p. 38)

1. You're going to sew on a button.
2. Cut a piece of thread.
3. Thread the needle.
4. Tie a knot at the end.
5. Stick the needle through the cloth.
6. Put it through a hole in the button.
7. Put it through the other hole.
8. Stick it back through the cloth.
9. Pull it tight.
10. Do it again and again.
11. Finish it.
12. Bite the thread off.

EXERCISE   SCRAMBLED SENTENCES

Answers to Exercise:
Same as the numbered sentences of the text above.

Before beginning this activity, cut out the pictures in the picture sequence and the sentences on the exercise sheet. With beginning students you can use the pictures and with more advanced students you can use the pictures and text. Put the pictures and/or the sentences in separate envelopes and divide the class into small groups. Ask the students in each group to arrange the pictures and/or sentences in order; then, have students match the sentences to the pictures.

As you circulate among the groups, check comprehension by asking questions such as "What did he do after he bit off the thread?" "What did he do after he threaded the needle?" or "Why can't you put *Stick the needle through the cloth* after *Thread the needle*?" Point to the pictures as you ask the questions. After all student groups have sequenced pictures and text, write one sentence from the text on the board and ask what sentences come before and after it. If you are using an overhead projector, arrange part of the picture sequence or text in order and leave out part. Ask students to tell you what is missing.

*Text for this sequence comes from page 17 of *Live Action English* by Elizabeth Romijn and Contee Seely (Berkeley, Calif.: Command Performance Language Institute, 1979, 1988, 1997) and is used with permission of the authors.

These activities are suggested for use with the *Sewing On a Button* picture sequence. Many of them may be suitable for use with other sequences as well. For additional suggestions, see *Extension Activities* (pp. viii–x).

Grammar

Can/Can't   Using props such as a needle, thread, and things that need mending (socks with holes, shirts without buttons, skirts without hems), have high beginning and intermediate students talk about themselves using *can* and *can't* (**Example:** "I can sew on a button, but I can't hem a skirt." "I can't thread a needle because my eyes are too bad."). Give students time to examine the props and decide what they can and can't do. Tell them they must give a reason for not being able to do something. (You can turn this activity into a chain game by having each student repeat all of the sentences and reasons given by preceding students).

Regular and irregular verbs   Ask your intermediate students to classify all of the verbs in the text as *regular* or *irregular* and to give the past participle of each as follows:

REGULAR	IRREGULAR
sew — sewed*	sew — sewn*
thread — threaded	cut — cut
finish — finished	stick — stuck
pull — pulled	put — put

Have students practice making affirmative and negative statements and questions with the verbs. Then, ask each student to write on three separate pieces of paper three questions using three different verbs. Mix the questions together in a bag or box and ask each student to draw three papers from it. The student must then answer the questions either orally or in writing.

Pronunciation

This picture sequence offers opportunity for students to practice pronouncing the voiceless /th/ and voiced /thr/ and the lateral /l/ in the initial, medial, and final positions.

Have students repeat these sentences:

"Thread the needle."
"Stick the needle through the cloth."

Have students practice these groups of words:

"through, thread, throw, three"
"thing, thin, think, cloth, with"
"the, this, other"

*The past participle for *sew* can be regular (*sewed*) or irregular (*sewn*).

Discussion

Intermediate and advanced students can engage in lively discussion about sex roles and stereotypes prompted by questions such as "Who does the sewing in your family?" and "Should boys be taught to sew or only girls?" "Why?" Ask students to comment on the household tasks they perform: mending, repairing, baking, cooking, plumbing, carpentry, etc. Use their answers as the basis for new TPR sequences related to the students' actual skills and experiences. Or have each student create a sequence to teach to the rest of the class. Possibilities include: polishing shoes; giving a haircut; sewing a hem; replacing a washer; changing a diaper; replacing a worn electrical plug; and so on.

Verb Lists

TAKING CARE OF BABY (p. 40)

1. take (care)
2. hold
3. is
4. kiss
5. hug
6. squeeze
7. offer
8. feed
9. spitting (out)
10. put (down)
11. clean (up)

PAINTING A PICTURE (p. 41)

1. paint
2. spread (out)
3. take (out)
4. open
5. pick (up)
6. dip
7. dry
8. close
9. put (away)
10. wash
11. wipe
12. hang
13. fold (up)

CHANGING A LIGHT BULB (p. 42)

1. turn (on)
2. is
3. change
4. go
5. get
6. unplug
7. take (off)
8. unscrew
9. screw
10. put (back) (on)
11. plug
12. work
13. throw (away)

PUTTING UP A TOWEL RACK (p. 43)

1. put (up) (down)
2. hold (up)
3. make
4. are (they're)
5. stick
6. screw
7. tighten

WRITING A LETTER (p. 44)

1. write
2. sign
3. fold (up)
4. put
5. lick
6. seal
7. tear (off)
8. stick
9. take
10. mail

WASHING DISHES (p. 45)

1. need (to)
2. wash
3. fill
4. squeeze
5. rinse
6. put
7. scrub
8. let (out)
9. sprinkle

DUSTING (p. 46)

1. get
2. go (into)
3. dust
4. are (you're)
5. forget (don't)
6. pick (off)
7. put (on)
8. clean
9. plug (in)
10. vacuum
11. is (it's)

TIME TO CLEAN HOUSE (p. 47)

1. is
2. put (on) (away)
3. sprinkle
4. scrub
5. sweep
6. fill
7. pour
8. stick
9. mop
10. dust
11. empty
12. plug
13. turn (on)
14. vacuum
15. look (around)

ICE CREAM AND TV (p. 48)

1. go (into) (back)
2. open
3. get (out)
4. close
5. put (away)
6. leave
7. turn (on)
8. sit
9. watch
10. eat
11. are (you're)
12. melted
13. forgot

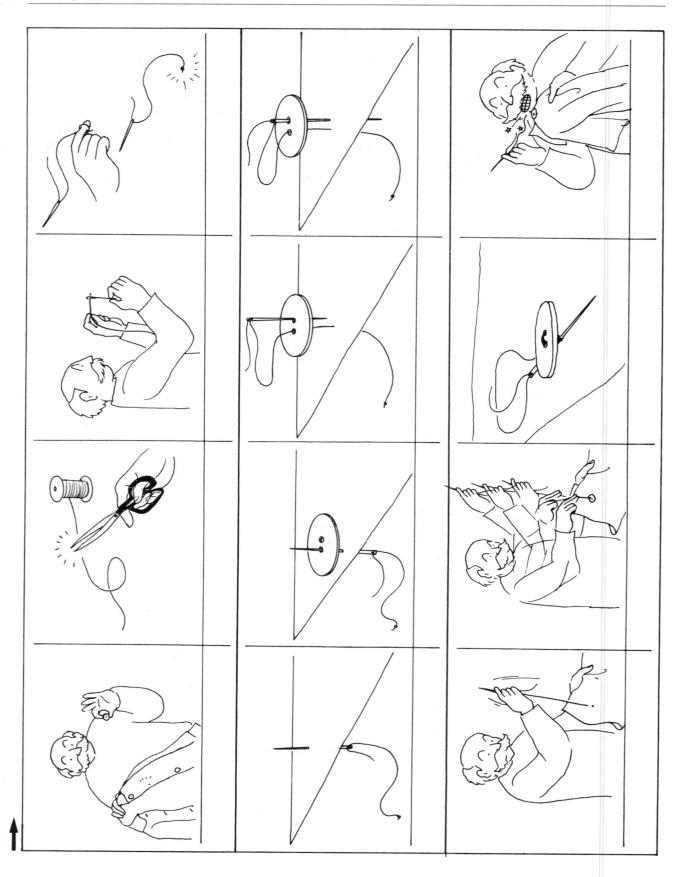

ACTION ENGLISH PICTURES   *UNIT 3 / AT HOME*

Scrambled Sentences

Sewing on a Button

Directions: Put these sentences in the correct order.

Thread the needle.

Pull it tight.

You're going to sew on a button.

Bite the thread off.

Cut a piece of thread.

Do it again and again.

Tie a knot at the end.

Stick it back through the cloth.

Put it through a hole in the button.

Finish it.

Put it through the other hole.

Stick the needle through the cloth.

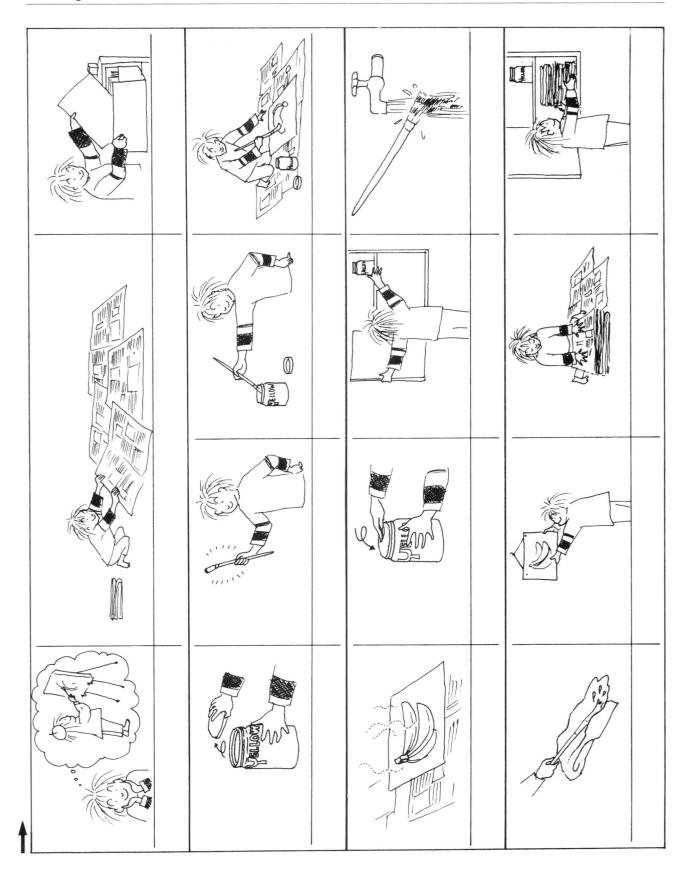

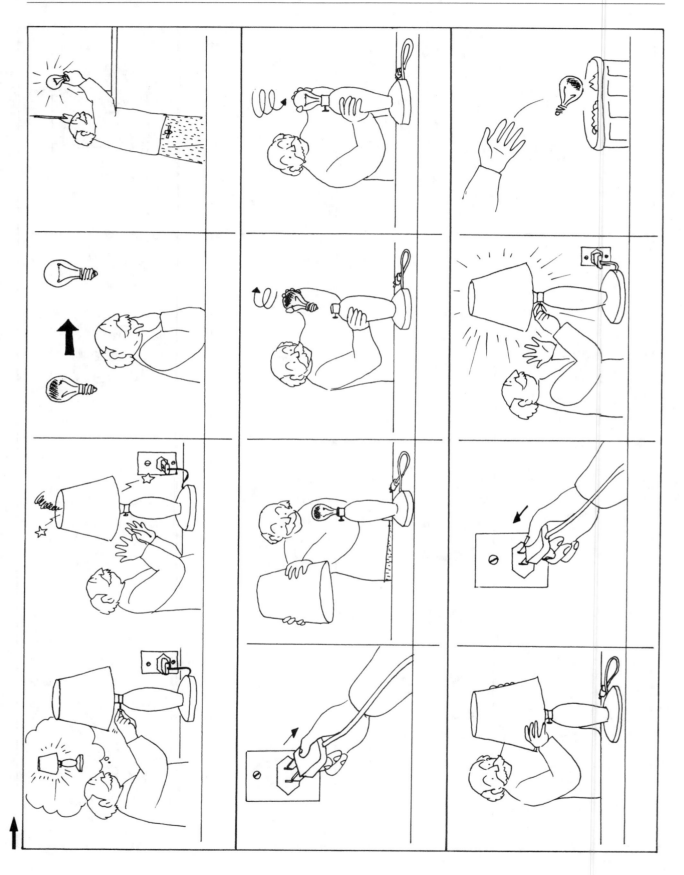

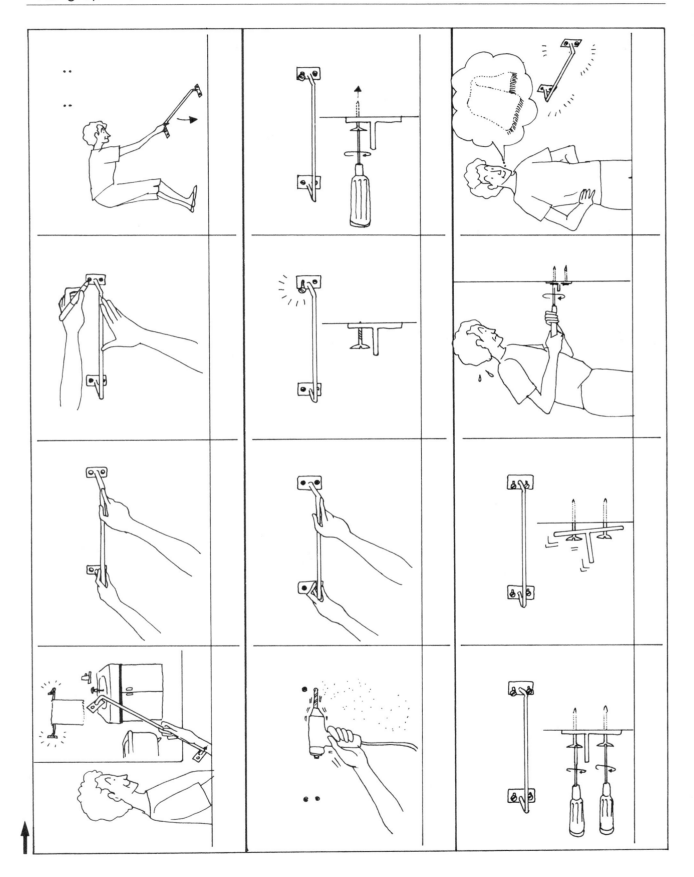

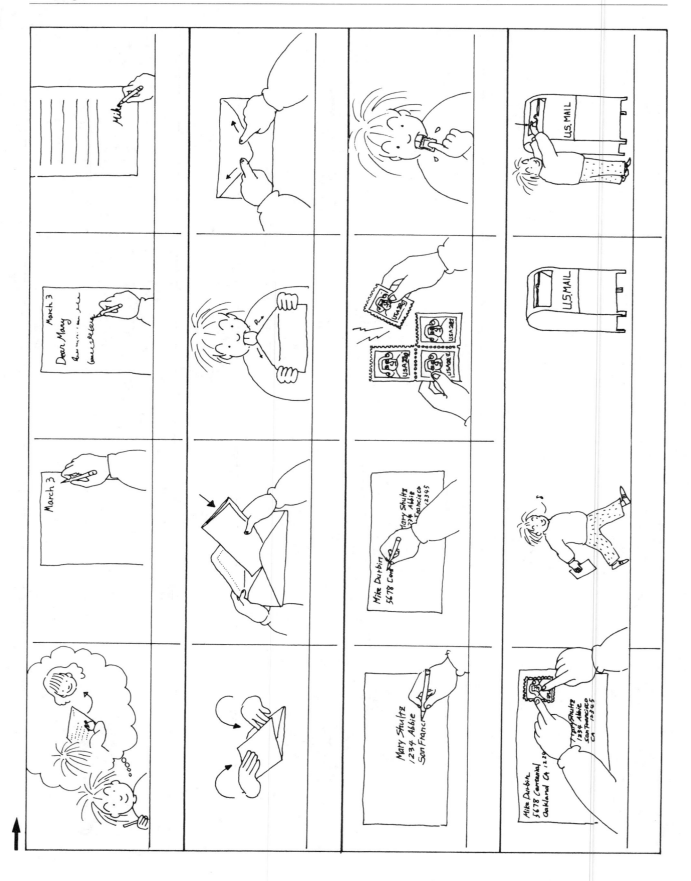

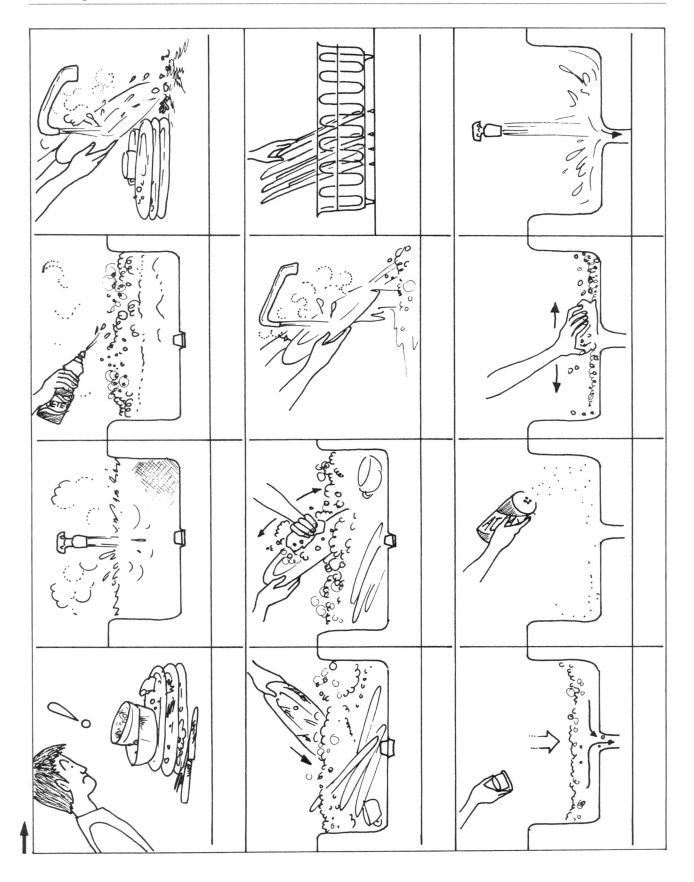

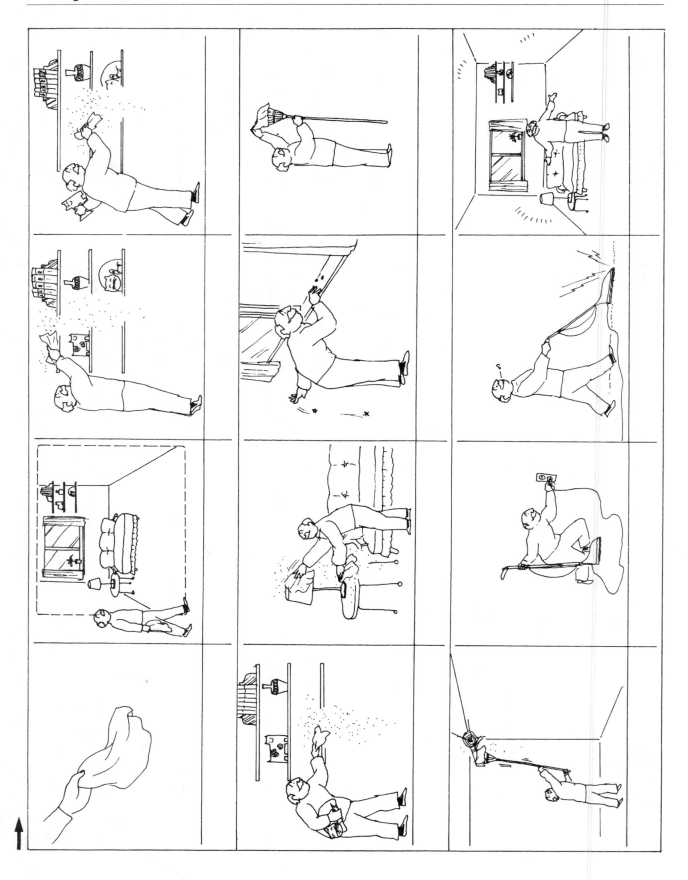

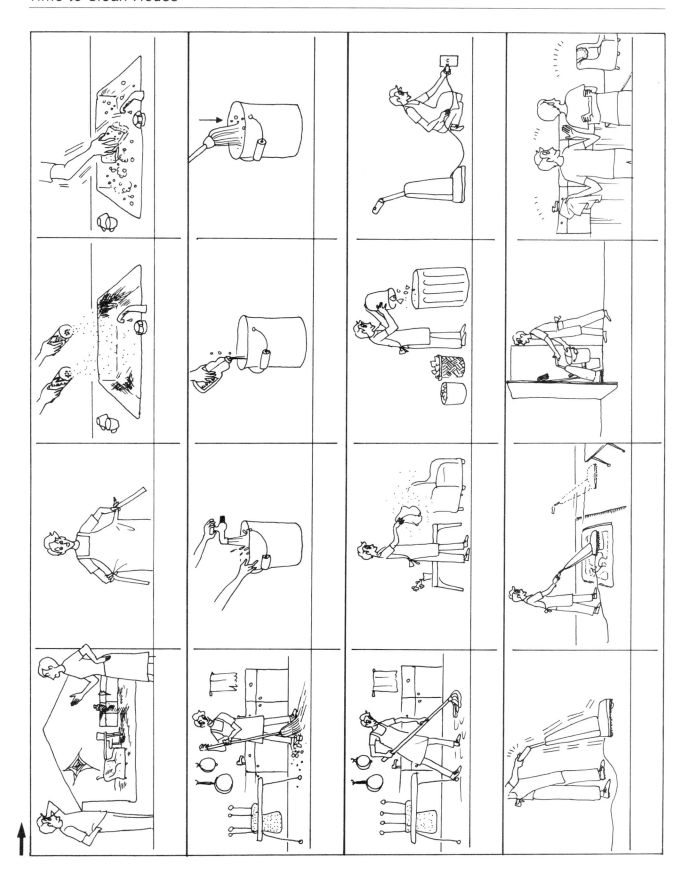

UNIT 4 **GOING OUT**

Model Lesson

Shopping for a Coat

Before presenting the model lesson, review the general procedure for using TPR (pp. vii–viii) to introduce the text below and picture sequence *Shopping for a Coat* (p. 54). When students are familiar with both the text and the pictures, make class copies of the reading exercise (p. 55).

LESSON TEXT

SHOPPING FOR A COAT*(p. 54)

1. You're going shopping for a new coat.
2. Look in the store window.
3. Oh! There's a nice coat. Go inside.
4. Take a coat off the rack.
5. Take it off the hanger.
6. Try it on.
7. Look at yourself in the mirror.
8. It's too big. Take it off.
9. Put it back on the hanger.
10. Hang it up.
11. Try on another one.
12. This one fits.
13. Look at the price tag.
14. How much is it?
15. Buy it.

EXERCISE

READING AND WRITING

Answers to Exercise:
1. A new coat.
2. On the second floor.
3. $75.00.
4. It's too big.
5. $50.00
6. It's on sale.

Have students first read the story through silently, then read it to them aloud. After you have read the story aloud, have students read it to you. Then, ask them to answer the comprehension questions first orally, then in writing.

Have your intermediate students change the verbs in the story from present to past tense. Give them a sentence to get them started: "When Anna Ray was 16 years old, she needed a new coat . . ." After students have rewritten the story, ask them to rewrite the comprehension questions or write new questions in the past tense. If students write new questions, have them exchange papers so that one student answers another student's questions. In this way, students learn whether or not their questions are comprehensible.

*Text for this sequence comes from page 11 of *Live Action English* by Elizabeth Romijn and Contee Seely (Berkeley, Calif.: Command Performance Language Institute, 1979, 1988, 1997) and is used with permission of the authors.

These activities are suggested for use with the *Shopping for a Coat* picture sequence. Many of them may be suitable for use with other sequences as well. For additional suggestions, see *Extension Activities* (pp. viii–x).

Grammar/Pronunciation

Once they have learned the text for *Shopping for a Coat,* have high beginning students repeat or read the text replacing the command form with the simple present tense and inserting the pronoun *I, she,* or *he.* You may want to write the sentences on the board first and rewrite the verbs and pronouns as they are replaced by other forms. Have students do this activity with you as a group and then with partners. Note the change in spelling for *try/tries,* the *s* in *look(s), take(s), put(s),* and the *es* in *go(es).* Practice pronunciation of these new verb forms. For the next to last line of the text, "How much is it?" add the words " she asks" before or after the question.

Roleplaying

This picture sequence is a perfect starting point for roleplaying shopping for clothes. Students will need vocabulary for talking about different kinds of clothing, sizes, and prices. Have your intermediate and advanced students develop dialogs to roleplay using such openers as "I'm looking for a . . ." "I need a . . ." "Could you tell me where the _____ are/is?" and so forth. Also practice ways of avoiding aggressive salesclerks: "Thank you, I'm just looking," or "I'd just like to look, thanks." Take the part of the salesclerk or assign it to a student to roleplay.

Vocabulary Building

When you present *Shopping for a Coat* as a TPR lesson, you can go beyond the given text to include or substitute different kinds of clothing that can be described in a variety of ways. To broaden your students' shopping vocabulary and familiarize them with American shopping customs, bring into class a bagful of clothing. Be sure to include articles of varying colors, shapes, styles, and sizes. Have students practice shopping for particular items such as striped ties, plaid shirts, long and short-sleeved blouses, polka-dotted, floral, printed, and plain dresses, full and straight skirts. Have students try on clothing for size to practice adjective forms: "This skirt's too big." "That one is smaller." "This skirt is too loose." "That one is tighter." "This dress is old-fashioned." "That one is more stylish." You can also practice pre-articles and counters with such words and phrases as *socks/pair of socks, slacks/pair of slacks, shoes/pair of shoes, pants/pair of pants.* The possibilities are numerous.

Discussion

A good discussion topic for more advanced students is a comparison-contrast of shopping practices in the U.S. and in other countries. Ask students about bargaining and how they feel about fixed prices. What was their best bargain? What do they think about thrift shopping and garage sales? Why do they suppose people shop at flea markets? If students have never gone to a garage sale or a flea market, perhaps you can arrange a class field trip.

Verb Lists

EATING OUT (p. 56)

1. want (to)	10. order
2. eat (out)	11. bring
3. decide	12. is (it's)
4. go	13. clear
5. follow	14. like
6. sit (down)	15. finish
7. look (over)	16. pay (for)
8. ask	17. forget (don't)
9. are	18. leave

USING A PAY PHONE (p. 57)

1. make	10. is (it's)
2. go (into)	11. hang (up)
3. check	12. get (back)
4. pick (up)	13. wait
5. take (out)	14. whistle
6. stick	15. try
7. listen (for)	16. ringing
8. hear	17. talk
9. dial	

GROCERY SHOPPING (p. 58)

1. are (you're)	7. stand
2. go	8. say
3. choose	9. pay
4. put (back)	10. wait
5. weigh	11. bag
6. is (that's)	12. pick (up)

AT THE LAUNDROMAT (p. 59)

1. do	7. wait (for)
2. sort	8. are (they're)
3. put	9. is (it's)
4. add	10. take (out)
5. set	11. finish
6. sit (down)	12. fold (up)

THE POST OFFICE (p. 60)

1. are (you're)	9. give
2. going (to)	10. tell
3. mail	11. want (to)
4. wait	12. weigh
5. smile	13. check
6. moving	14. cost
7. is	15. say
8. take	16. leave

THE BANK (p. 61)

1. cash	7. wait
2. walk (into) (up)	8. move
	9. hand
3. go (over) (out)	10. say
	11. take
4. write	12. count
5. sign	13. put (away)
6. get	

A HAIRCUT (p. 62)

1. getting, get (up)	9. chat
2. need	10. watch
3. go	11. work
4. is	12. look (at)
5. have	13. done
6. wait	14. pay
7. read	15. give
8. sit	

A ROUGH BUS RIDE (p. 63)

1. are (you're)	12. look (out)
2. waiting (for)	13. bounce
3. come	14. watch (for)
4. get (on) (up) (off)	15. ring
5. pay	16. stand (up)
6. ask (for)	17. stop
7. is	18. go
8. fall (down)	19. step (down)
9. tell	20. push
10. take	21. wipe
11. sit (down)	22. say

TAKING THE PLANE (p. 64)

1. going, go	8. tighten
2. get (on)	9. taking off
3. look (for)	10. flying (through)
4. sit	
5. fasten	11. unfasten
6. is (it's) (that's)	12. are (we're)
7. loosen	13. enjoy

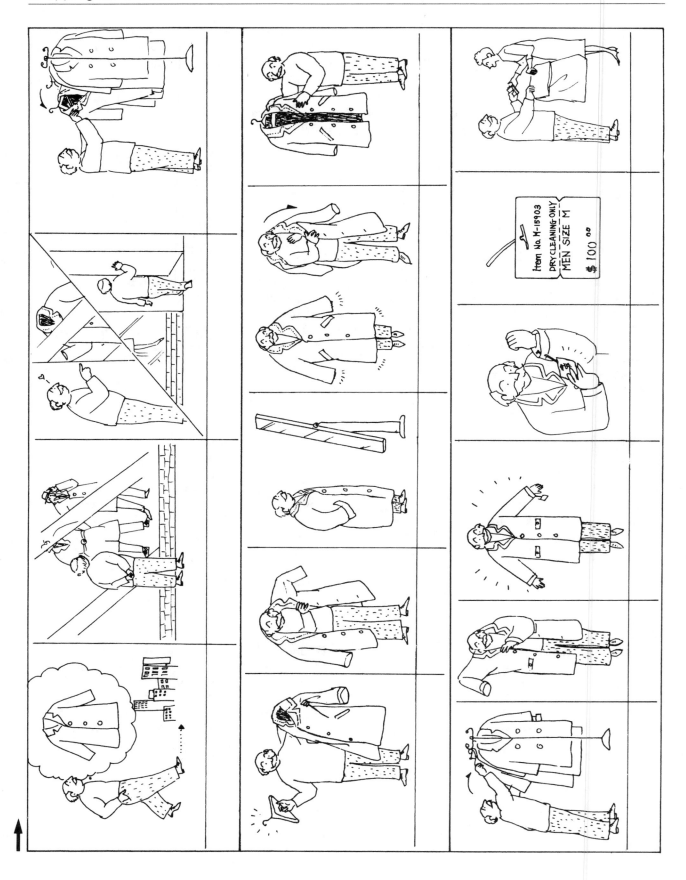

Reading and Writing

Shopping for a Coat

Directions: Read the story and answer the questions.

Anna Ray is 16 years old. She needs a new coat. She is going shopping with her mother. They go to a big shopping center because there are many stores there.

At the shopping center they go into a big department store. The Girls' Coat Department is on the second floor. They take the escalator up to the second floor.

In the coat department, they see some coats on a coat rack. Anna wants a brown coat. She only has $75.00 to spend. She wants a coat that isn't expensive.

There are many nice coats on the rack. She looks at the price tags. The coats are not too expensive. She sees one she likes. She takes it off the hanger. She gives the hanger to her mother to hold. She tries on the coat and looks at herself in the mirror. The coat is too big. She takes it off and puts it back on the hanger. Her mother hangs it up.

Anna looks for another coat. She sees one she likes. She tries it on and looks at herself in the mirror again. She likes it. It fits perfectly. She looks at the price tag. The coat's only $50.00. It's on sale! Fantastic! She buys it.

1. What does Anna need?

_____

2. Where is the coat department for girls' coats?

_____

3. How much money does Anna have to spend?

_____

4. What's wrong with the first coat she tries on?

_____

5. How much does she spend on her new coat?

_____

6. Why is the coat cheap?

_____

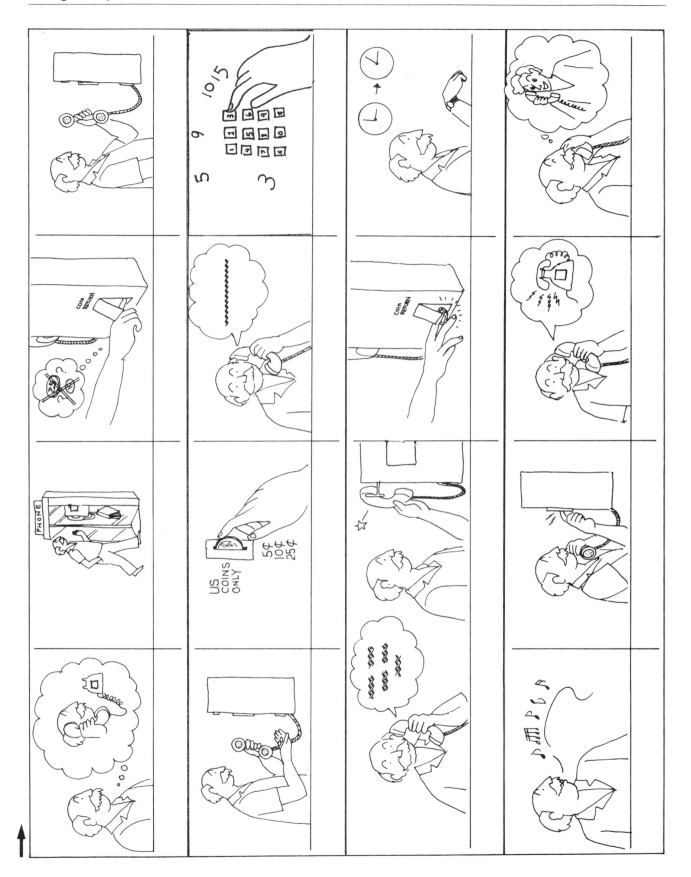

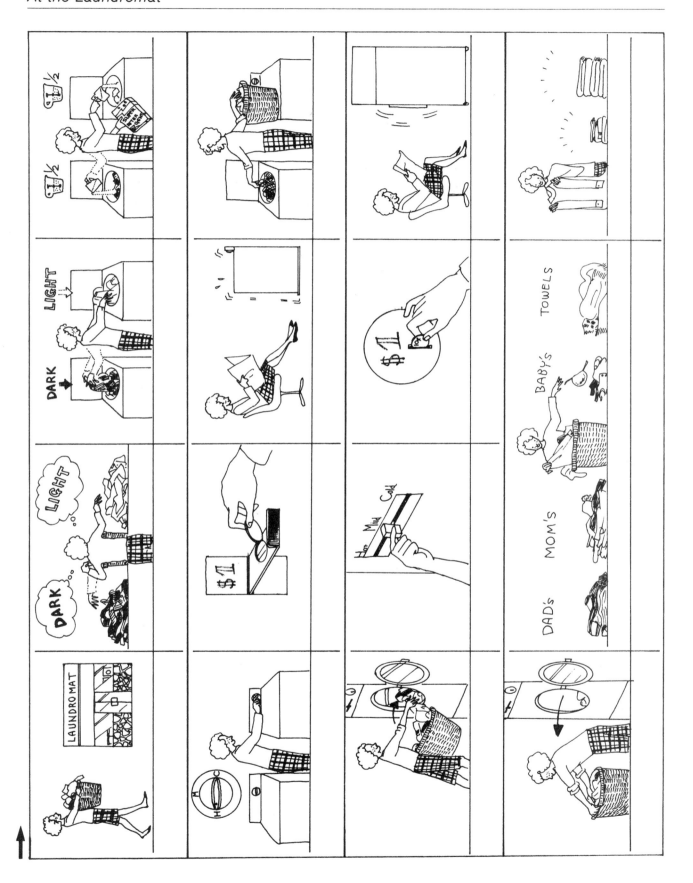

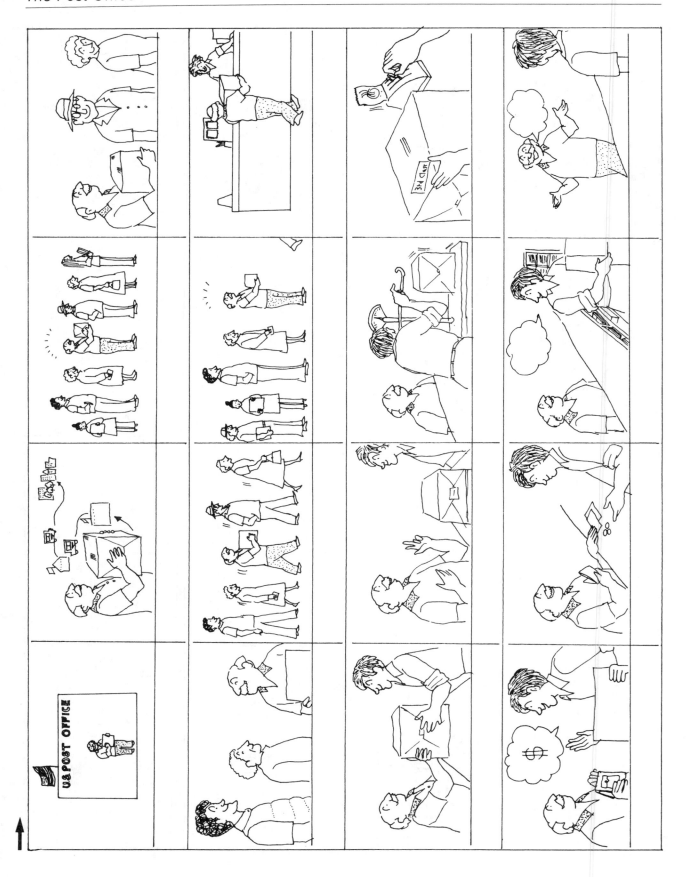

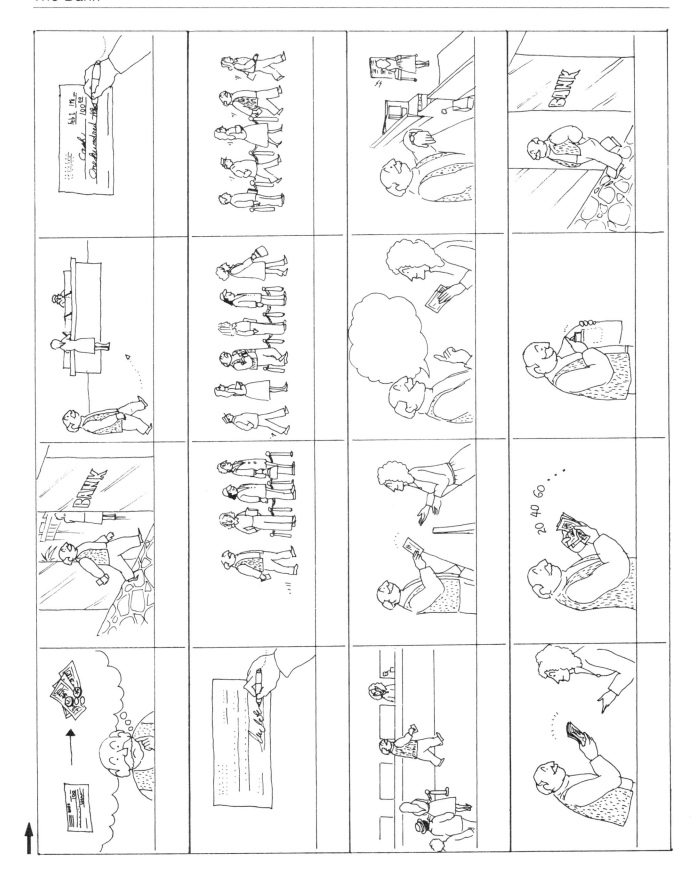

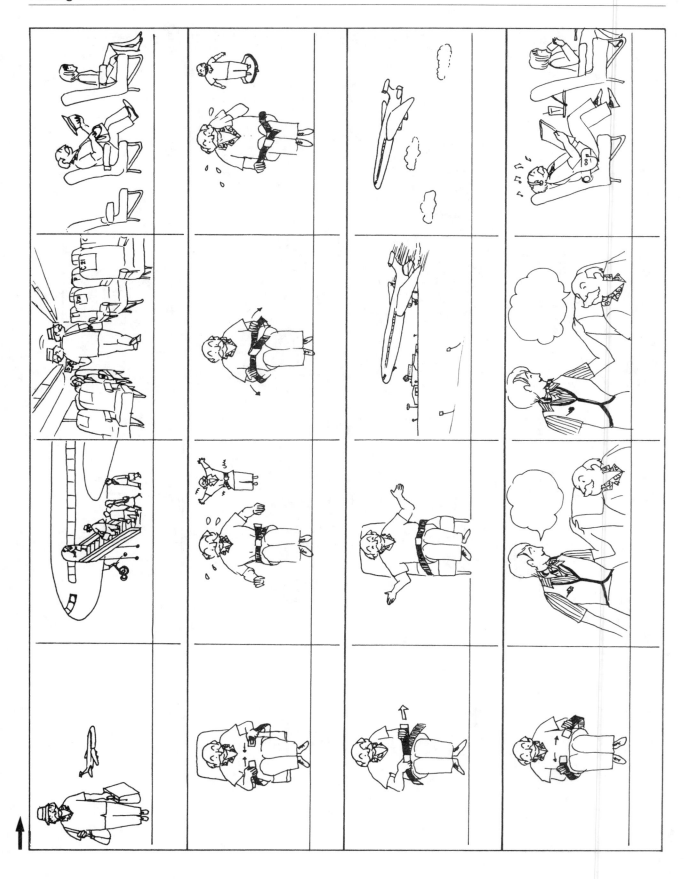

UNIT 5 **HOLIDAYS AND LEISURE**

Opening a Present
A Jack-O-Lantern for Halloween
A Thanksgiving Feast
Christmas
Valentine's Day
Wrapping a Present
A Sunday Drive
Going to the Movies
At the Beach
Taking Pictures

Model Lesson

Opening a Present

Before presenting the model lesson, review the general procedure for using TPR (pp. vii–viii) to introduce the text below and the picture sequence *Opening a Present* (p. 70). When students are familiar with both the text and the pictures, make class copies of the exercise sheet (p. 71).

LESSON TEXT — OPENING A PRESENT *(p. 70)

1. You got a present from your friend!
2. Look it over.
3. Feel it.
4. Shake it and listen to it.
5. Guess what's inside.
6. Tear off the paper.
7. Wad it up and throw it away.
8. Open the box just a little.
9. Peek inside.
10. Wow! It's just what you wanted.
11. Open the box and take it out.
12. Say, "Oh, thank you!"

EXERCISE — VERB PRACTICE

Answers to Exercise:
1. Look it over.
2. Shake it.
3. Feel it.
4. Open it.

Have beginning students first identify the action depicted in each picture frame and then find the verb that corresponds to that action. (Some students will need help in sounding out the words.) Tell students to draw a line from the picture to the verb phrase. When they have completed the matching activity, ask students to demonstrate different actions that are appropriate for gift-giving, such as "Untie the ribbon," "Tear open the package," "Lift off the lid," etc. If students don't know the names of the actions, help them by modeling the words and writing them on the board.

With intermediate and advanced students, try playing "What Can You Do With . . .?" Divide the class into small groups of four or five students. Ask each group to choose one person as its "recorder." Tell the groups that you will name an object and that they are to think of as many verbs as they can to associate with it. (Don't name the object until you are ready to begin!) Set a time limit (three minutes works well; two minutes adds excitement) and start everyone at the same time. At the end of the time, have each "recorder" read his/her group's list to the class. All verbs must be defensible by student explanation to be acceptable. The group with the most acceptable verbs

*Text for this sequence comes from page 22 of *Live Action English* by Elizabeth Romijn and Contee Seely (Berkeley, Calif.: Command Performance Language Institute, 1979, 1988, 1997) and is used with permission of the authors.

on its list wins. A variation of this game can be played with individual students listing verbs for various objects. Some good words for association are: *apple, piano, husband, cow, newspaper, child, job, cigarette, baby, rice, money, criminal.*

ADDITIONAL ACTIVITIES READING CHECKS, DISCUSSION

These activities are suggested for use with the *Opening a Present* picture sequence. Many of them may be suitable for use with other sequences as well. For additional suggestions, see *Extension Activities* (pp. viii–x).

Reading Checks

Beginning-reading comprehension checks can be done by students in a number of ways: using cloze readings, making choices, correcting something, arranging a story in sequence. Here are two fast and easy checking activities suitable for beginning and low intermediate students:

What's the Word? Select the correct word in parentheses ( ).

1. You got a present from your (friend/box).
2. Look it (up/over).
3. (Guess/Peek) what's inside.
4. Wad up the paper and (take/throw) it away.
5. (Open/Close) the box just a little.
6. Wow! It's (just/isn't) what you wanted.

What's Wrong? Correct the story*.

You got a bomb from your friend. Look it back. Feel it. Shake it and hit it. Guess what's inside. Tear off your friend. Wad him up and throw him away. Close the box just a little. Peek-a-boo. Wow! It isn't what you wanted. Open the box and take it outside. Say, "Oh, no, thank you!"

Discussion

This picture sequence provides an opportunity for students to discuss gift-giving practices and the language associated with giving and receiving gifts.

With beginning students, practice roleplaying receiving a gift with phrases such as "Thank you," "Thank you so much," "Oh, thank you!" "You shouldn't have," "How kind of you!" "What a surprise!" and "I can't thank you enough." With more advanced students, discuss cultural differences involving gift-giving practices. (For example, people from some cultures do not open their gifts in front of the giver, whereas Americans tend to immediately acknowledge the gift.)

*Thanks to fellow teacher Kristin Bach for this story from one of her lessons.

Discuss the occasions when gifts are given or exchanged and the kinds of gifts that are appropriate. Ask your students about their native customs and celebrations. Compare cultural practices surrounding birthdays, weddings, anniversaries, births, deaths, and so forth.

Verb Lists

A JACK-O-LANTERN FOR HALLOWEEN (p. 72)

1. carve
2. cut (off) (out)
3. take (off)
4. clean (out) (up)
5. light
6. wait (for)
7. melt
8. drip
9. stick
10. put (on)

A THANKSGIVING FEAST (p. 73)

1. have
2. set
3. take (out)
4. put
5. call
6. is (it's)
7. sit (down)
8. say
9. carve
10. serve
11. pass
12. eat
13. am

CHRISTMAS (p. 74)

1. is (it's)
2. wrap
3. sing
4. put
5. bake
6. write
7. hang (up)
8. leave
9. tuck
10. wake (up)
11. pick (up)
12. shake
13. unwrap
14. play
15. have
16. say

VALENTINE'S DAY (p. 75)

1. is (it's)
2. want (to)
3. give
4. get
5. fold
6. draw
7. cut
8. unfold
9. write
10. say

WRAPPING A PRESENT (p. 76)

1. wrap (up) (around)
2. put
3. fold
4. tape
5. cut
6. tie
7. make
8. give

A SUNDAY DRIVE (p. 77)

1. are (you're)
2. going (for)
3. start
4. look (behind) (in front of)
5. pull (out) (into)
6. drive (through) (over)
7. slow (down)
8. signal
9. turn (on)
10. count
11. look (at) (for)
12. want (to)
13. get (out)
14. stop
15. take

GOING TO THE MOVIES (p. 78)

1. go (to) (into)
2. buy
3. give
4. open
5. look (for)
6. is (here's)
7. sit (down)
8. watch
9. smile
10. wipe
11. scream
12. laugh
13. clap
14. get (up)
15. leave
16. like

AT THE BEACH (p. 79)

1. is (it's)
2. are (you're)
3. unfold
4. sit (down)
5. put (on)
6. look (at)
7. stare (at)
8. watch
9. smile
10. sweating
11. stand (up)
12. take (off)
13. run (into) (back) (toward)
14. cool off
15. jump
16. come
17. dive
18. swim
19. have

TAKING PICTURES (p. 80)

1. take
2. load
3. wind
4. use
5. tell
6. stand
7. look (through)
8. spread (out)
9. sit (down)
10. move (over)
11. get
12. smile
13. press
14. stay

Verb Practice

Opening a Present

1.

2.

3.

4.

Directions: Draw a line from each picture to the sentence it matches.

What can you do with a present?

Feel it.

Open it.

Look it over.

Shake it.

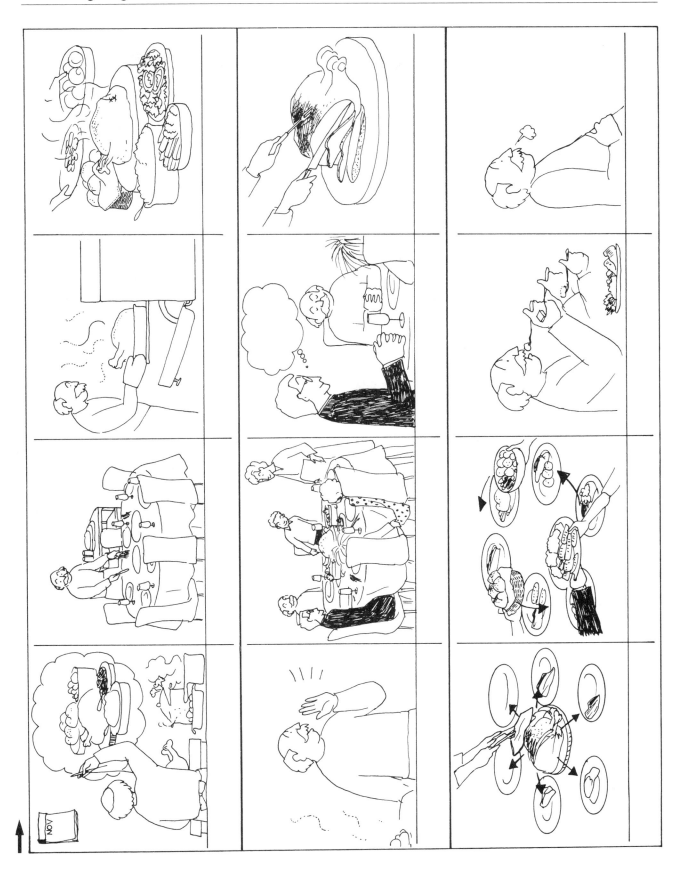

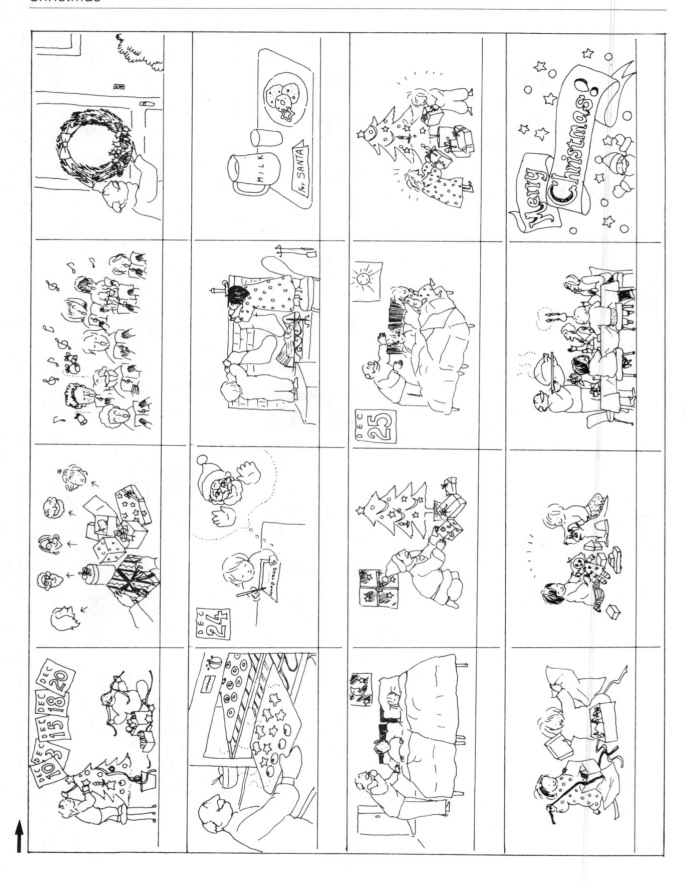

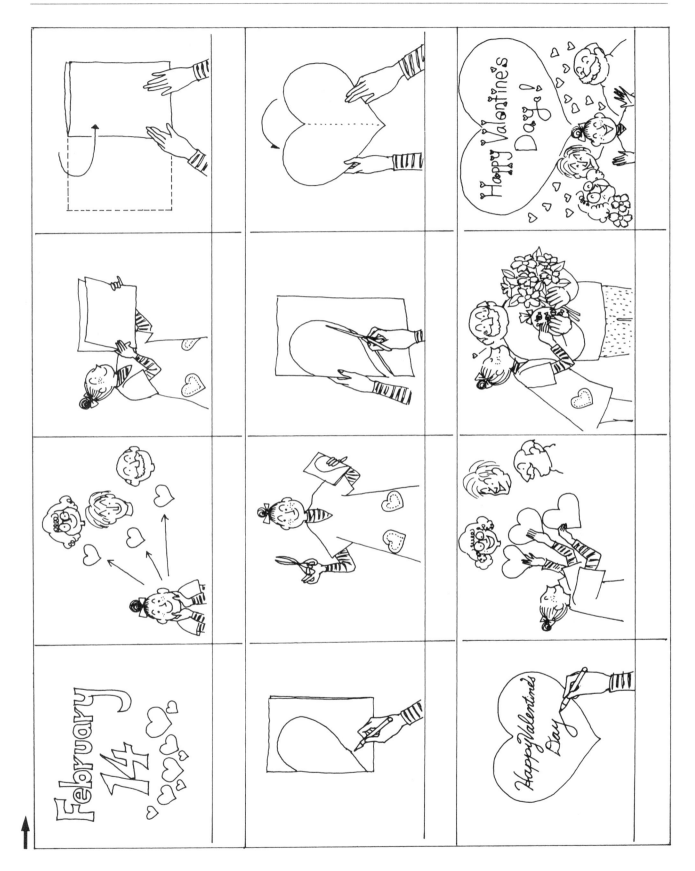

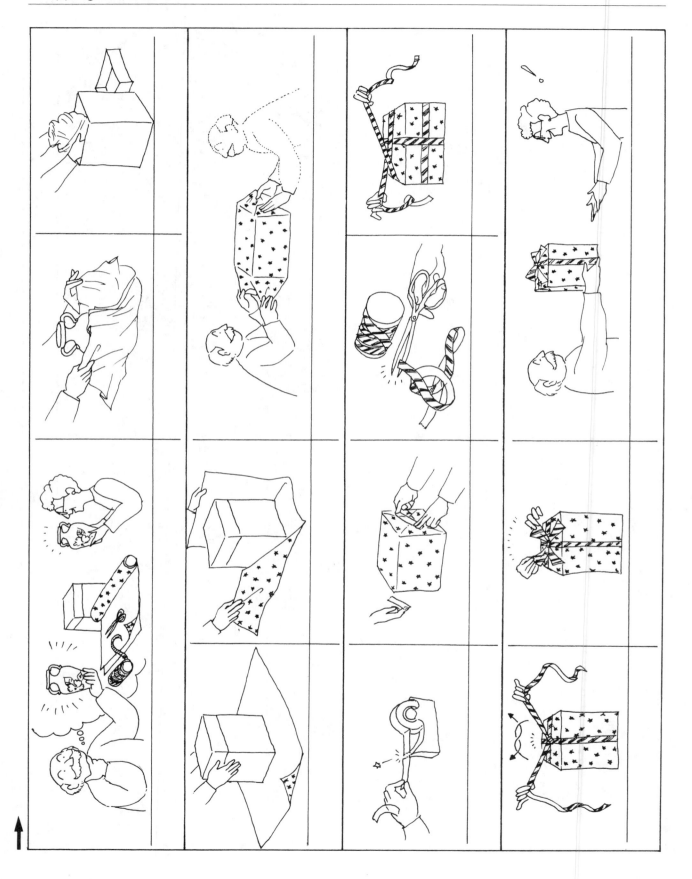

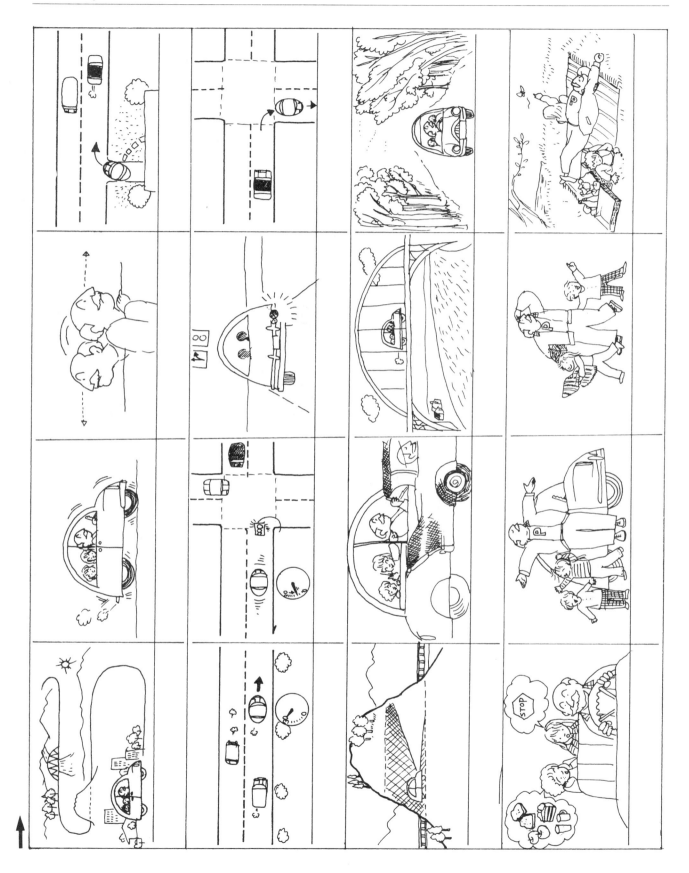

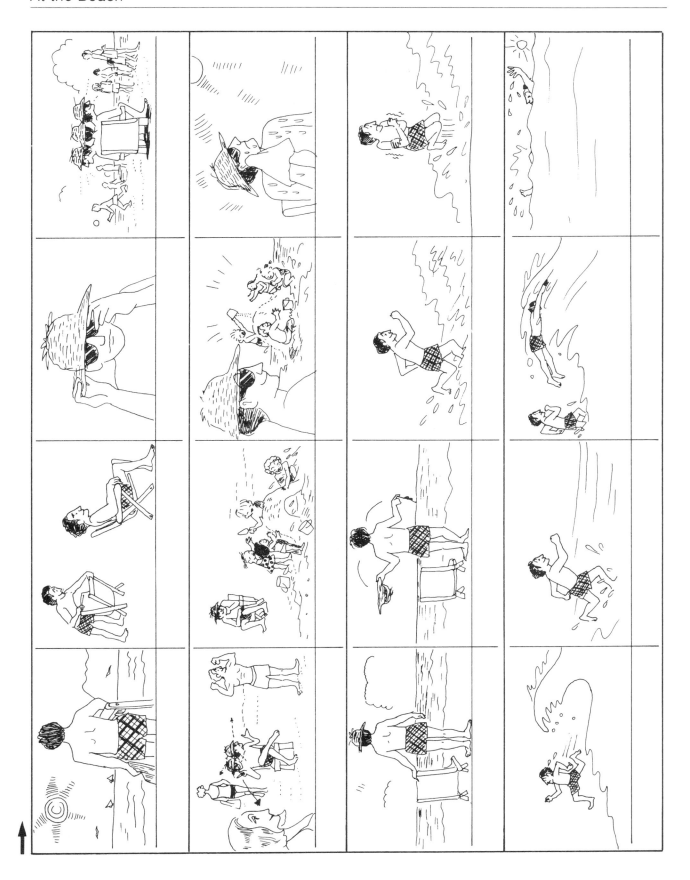

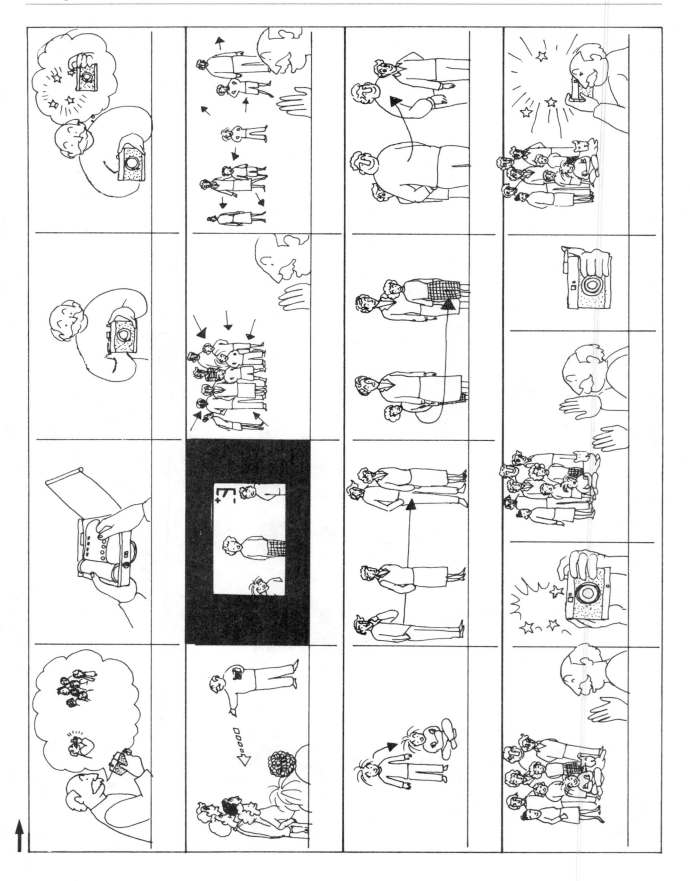

UNIT 6 **AT SCHOOL**

Model Lesson

Doing Homework

Before presenting the model lesson, review the general procedure for using TPR (pp. vii–viii) to introduce the text below and the picture sequence *Doing Homework* (p. 86). When students are familiar with both the text and the pictures, make class copies of the exercise sheet (p. 87).

LESSON TEXT | DOING HOMEWORK (p. 86)

1. You have a lot of homework today.
2. Get your books, paper, and pencil ready.
3. Sit down to study.
4. Open your book.
5. You're hungry. Go get an apple.
6. Go back to your homework.
7. Your favorite TV program is on.
8. Go watch TV.
9. The program is over.
10. Go back to your homework.
11. You want to listen to music.
12. Turn on the radio.
13. The music is great! Dance around.
14. It's getting late. You have to get to work.
15. Sit down and do your homework.
16. Finally, you're finished.
17. Put your stuff away.

EXERCISE | QUESTIONS AND ANSWERS

Answers to Exercise:
1. Why is he getting up/going to the kitchen?
2. Why is he watching TV?
3. Why is he turning on the radio?
4. Why is he dancing?
5. Why is he putting his books/things away?

Using the pictures from *Doing Homework,* have students practice responding to questions you pose. To make sure all students receive practice, make this an oral drill and move from one picture to the next, one student to the next. Point to the picture sequence as you ask questions. **For example:**

Teacher: "What does he have today?"
Student 1: "Homework."
Teacher: "What does he get ready?"
Student 2: "His paper, books, and pencil." (And so on.)

With beginning students, be careful not to mix question forms (Yes/No with WH— questions) until students have had sufficient practice with each form.

After students have had some practice in answering questions, select one picture from the sequence and ask several questions about it. **For example:**

Teacher: "Where is he going?"
Student 1: "To get an apple," or "To the kitchen."
Teacher: "What is he thinking about?"
Student 2: "An apple." (And so on.)

You can change the question from *he* to *you* to *we,* or from the present tense to the past to the continuous.

After modeling the questions for students to answer, ask the students to pose questions to each other, first as a class, then in pairs or small groups. Follow up with students dictating questions for you to write on the board or on a transparency.

Distribute copies of the worksheet (p. 87) and have students write both questions and answers. Since Why questions allow for multiple answers, have students practice giving more than one acceptable answer to each question.

Have high beginning or intermediate students write, on separate sheets of paper, as many questions as they can about each picture on the worksheet. Then, have students exchange papers and try to answer each others' questions to see whether or not they are clearly written.

You can also have teams of three or four students compete to see how many questions each team can write for a particular picture or set of pictures.

ADDITIONAL ACTIVITIES   GRAMMAR, ROLEPLAYING, DISCUSSION

These activities are suggested for use with the *Doing Homework* picture sequence. Many of them may be suitable for use with other sequences as well. For additional suggestions, see *Extension Activities* (pp. viii–x).

Grammar

Should/shouldn't   You can use the model lesson worksheet (p. 87) to practice modals of obligation and advisability. Use an overhead projector or delete the original instructions on the worksheet and tell your students to write sentences using *should* and *shouldn't*. Have students work individually or in small groups writing advice on good study habits for the student pictured. Ask each group to think of at least five suggestions starting with "He should . . ." or "He shouldn't . . .". Some words you might introduce are: *concentrate, procrastinate, avoid, self-control, distractions*. Some idioms to introduce are: *stick with it, put your nose to the grindstone, get down to business, fool around, waste time, put off*.

Roleplaying

Have students write and roleplay dialogs between a concerned parent and the student pictured. What would a concerned parent say? What would an angry parent say? Use some of these openers:

Concerned parent:	"I'm really concerned about . . ."
	"It bothers me to see you . . ."
	"I'd like to talk to you about . . ."
Angry parent:	"Enough is enough!"
	"That does it!"
	"How many times do I have to tell you . . .?"
	"Now listen, . . ."

Discussion

A common human tendency is to avoid doing what is boring, tiresome, or difficult. Talk with your students about avoidance (procrastination) and why people avoid doing some things. Ask students what they put off or avoid doing. (Remember to point out the use of the V + ing gerund form following *put off* and *avoid* if you make this a grammar lesson.) Have students interview each other to find out what each avoids doing and what each does instead (sleeps, reads, eats, watches TV, etc.). Do a class survey to discover the most creative and most frequent avoidance behaviors. Have students chart the most commonly avoided tasks and the most popular distractions.

Verb Lists

SHARPENING YOUR PENCIL (p. 88)

1. pick (up)
2. look (at)
3. feel
4. is (it's)
5. want
6. borrow
7. stick
8. sharpen
9. clean
10. give (back)
11. write

GETTING READY FOR A TEST (p. 89)

1. have (to)
2. study
3. get
4. sit (down)
5. open
6. read
7. close
8. repeat
9. check
10. remember
11. underline
12. think (about)
13. ask
14. is
15. answer
16. know
17. relax
18. need
19. dream (about)

TAKING A TEST (p. 90)

1. have
2. are (you're)
3. look (at)
4. is
5. take
6. put (away)
7. remember (can't)
8. sweating
9. tell
10. relax
11. exhale
12. go (ahead)
13. answer

SICK AT SCHOOL (p. 91)

1. are (you're)
2. sitting
3. feel (don't)
4. rest
5. ask
6. tell
7. write
8. is (what's) (it's)
9. say
10. ache
11. have
12. take
13. call
14. come
15. pick (up)
16. go

LATE TO CLASS (p. 92)

1. are (you're), am (I'm), is
2. hurry
3. drop
4. pick (up)
5. stop
6. open
7. listening
8. tiptoe
9. turn
10. look (at)
11. blush
12. say
13. smile
14. sit (down)
15. coming

TAKING A BREAK (p. 93)

1. are (you're)
2. is (it's)
3. get (up)
4. stretch
5. leave
6. go (out)
7. lean
8. talk
9. want
10. sit (down)
11. eat
12. laugh
13. joke
14. look (at)
15. hurry (back)
16. made it (idiomatic)

GOING TO THE LIBRARY (p. 94)

1. return
2. go
3. take
4. check
5. is
6. have (to)
7. look (at) (over)
8. pay
9. like
10. choose
11. want (to)
12. ask
13. find
14. pick (out)
15. check (out)
16. show
17. let
18. say

Questions and Answers

Doing Homework

Directions: Write questions for the pictures below, beginning with *Why.* (**Example:** "Why is he getting his books and paper ready?")

1. _____
_____
_____

2. _____
_____
_____

3. _____
_____
_____

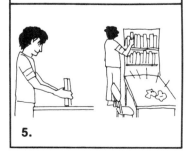

4. _____
_____
_____

5. _____
_____
_____

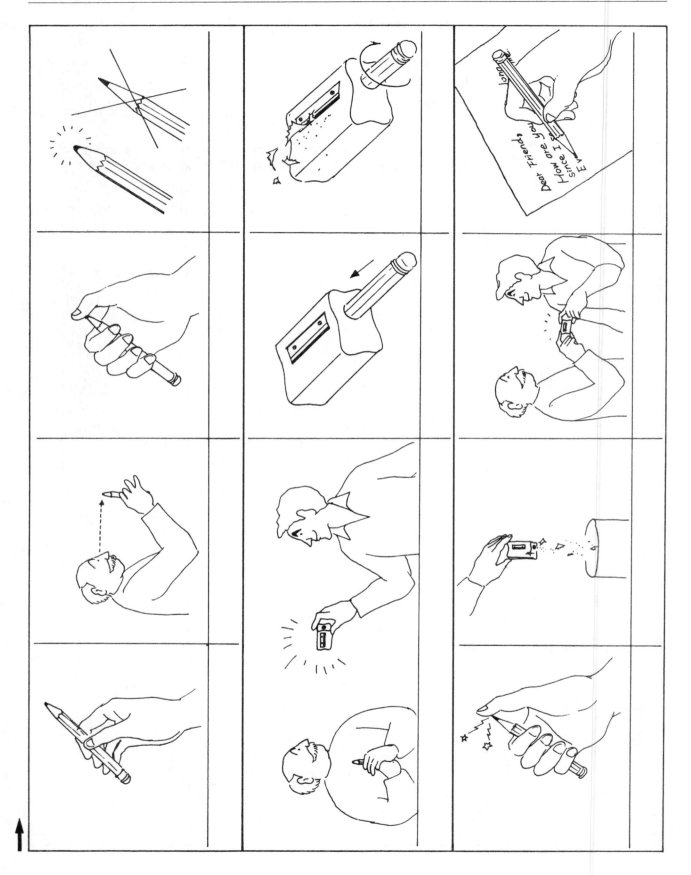

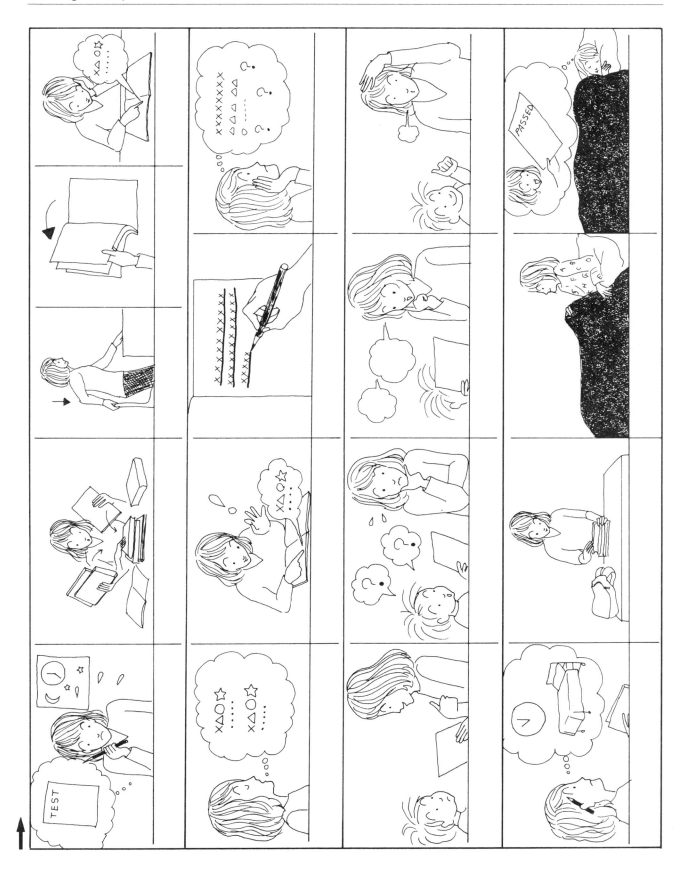

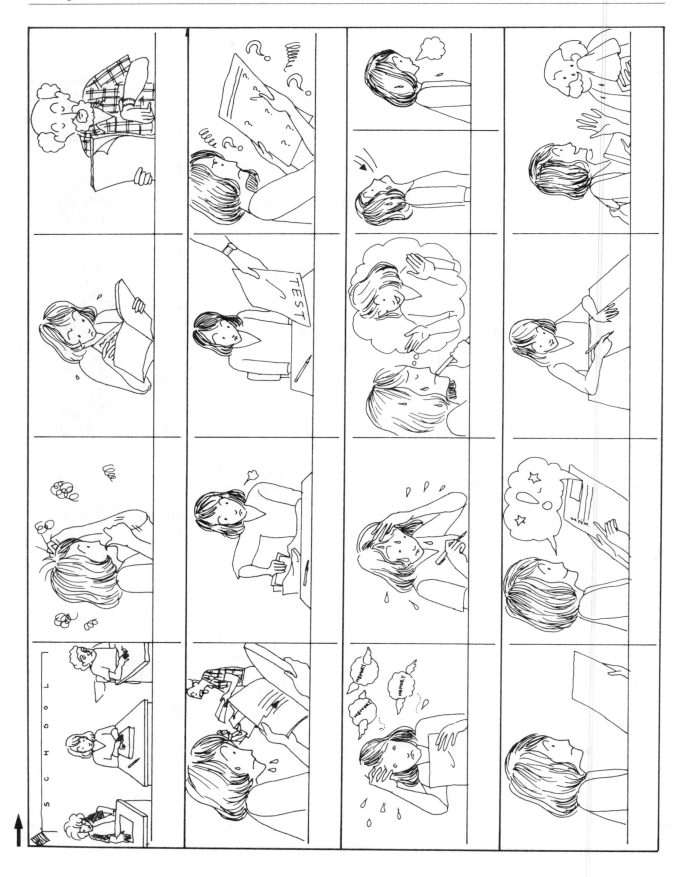

UNIT 7 **WEATHER**

Model Lesson

A Lost Umbrella

Before presenting the model lesson, review the general procedure for using TPR (pp. vii–viii) to introduce the text below and the picture sequence *A Lost Umbrella* (p. 101). When students are familiar with both the text and the pictures, make class copies of the exercise sheet (p. 102).

LESSON TEXT   A LOST UMBRELLA (p. 101)

1. It's raining outside.
2. You need your umbrella.
3. You can't find it.
4. Look in the closet. It isn't there.
5. Look under the table. It isn't there.
6. Look under the chair. It isn't there.
7. Look on top of the bookcase. It isn't there.
8. Look under the newspapers. It isn't there.
9. Move the sofa.
10. Look behind the sofa. It isn't there.
11. You can't find it.
12. You're late for work.
13. You have to go.
14. Put on your hat.
15. Open the door.
16. Oh, there it is, on the porch.
17. You found it.

EXERCISE   PREPOSITIONS

Answers to Exercise:
1. Look in the closet.
2. Look under the chair.
3. Look behind the sofa.
4. Look under the table.
5. Look on top of the bookcase.
6. Look under the newspapers.

This picture sequence is especially useful for teaching prepositions and vocabulary about the house. Additional prepositions that may be included in the exercise are: *in back of, underneath, through (the newspapers), next to, in front of.* You can also add different places in the house where students might look for something: on top of the refrigerator, next to the TV, behind the chair, on the hook in the closet, underneath the bed, and so on.

Before distributing the exercise sheet, write this sentence pattern on the board:

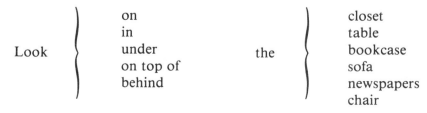

Look   on / in / under / on top of / behind   the   closet / table / bookcase / sofa / newspapers / chair

Have beginning students orally create sentences according to the pattern; then dictate sentences from the chart for students to write. Write the correct sentence on the board before you dictate the next sentence so that students receive immediate feedback. Once students understand how to use the chart, give them the exercise sheet to complete.

Ask your high beginning or low intermediate students to write sentences suggesting where to look for these items: a missing shoe (under the bed, next to the dog, under a table); a hat (on the shelf in the closet, under a coat, on your head); a lipstick (in a purse, in front of the mirror, on the dresser, underneath some tissue); and any other items commonly misplaced. Ask your students what they most frequently lose and where they can expect to find it.

ADDITIONAL ACTIVITIES

HIDE AND SEEK, ROLEPLAYING, PRONUNCIATION

These activities are suggested for use with *A Lost Umbrella* picture sequence. Many of them may be suitable for use with other sequences as well. For additional suggestions, see *Extension Activities* (pp. viii–x).

Hide and Seek

Send two students out of the classroom. With the remaining students, decide where to hide an umbrella in the classroom. The hiding place should be reasonable so that students can describe it without too much difficulty. Hide the umbrella, then call the two students back into the room. Have one student tell the other where to look for the lost umbrella. The second student must respond after looking where directed. **For example:**

> *Student A*: "Look behind the teacher's desk."
> *Student B* (after looking): "It isn't there."

It's a good idea to set a time limit (three minutes is enough) and encourage the rest of the class to provide help: "You're getting closer," "You're close," "You're too far," and so on. When the two students find the umbrella, they can choose two other students to replace them and repeat the game.

Roleplaying

A Lost Umbrella provides students with the opportunity to practice offering suggestions to one another. Create (or ask students to think of) situations in which someone is looking for something, deciding to buy something, or wondering what to do, and someone else offers suggestions. Try these phrases as roleplay openers: "Why don't you . . .?" "How about . . .?" "Do you think . . .?" "Have you tried . . .?" or "Maybe you should . . ."

Here are some situations for your students to roleplay:

1. Your friend misplaced a prescription for some medicine s/he needs. Offer some suggestions about where s/he might look.

2. Your sister wants to buy a pair of earrings for a friend. Offer some suggestions about where she might find some.
3. A good friend tells you s/he has received a letter from friends in his/her native country. They want to send their 15-year-old daughter to stay with him/her for two months. Your friend has a large family and a small apartment. Offer some suggestions.

After roleplaying a few dialogs, have students write about their own experiences losing something. Ask students to read their stories aloud and have other students offer suggestions about what to do, using the dialog openers. Be sure students change the verbs to the past tense if they are discussing a previous problem or experience.

Pronunciation

On the/under the   Beginning students often have problems with the phrases *on the* and *under the*. Practice aurally first by having students respond to commands such as "Put the pencil on the table/under the table." (Tapping a pencil to demonstrate the syllabic differences sometimes helps.) After students have practiced discriminating between the two phrases, have them do the following written exercise in pairs:

PARTNER A

Directions: Read sentence a. or b. to your partner.

1a. Write your name on the line.
 b. Write your name under the line.

2a. Draw a circle around the ▲ under the line.
 b. Draw a circle around the ▲ on the line.

3a. Draw a man standing on the line.
 b. Draw a man standing under the line.

4a. Draw a bird on the tree.
 b. Draw a bird under the tree.

5a. Point to the apple on the table.
 b. Point to the apple under the table.

PARTNER B

Directions: Listen as your partner reads a sentence. Then, do what the sentence tells you.

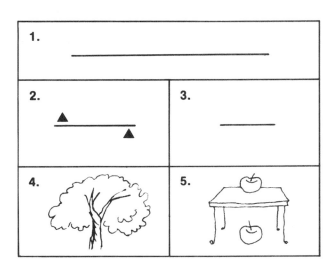

Verb Lists

A RAINY DAY (p. 103)

1. are (you're)
2. walking
3. is (there's)
4. stop, stopped
5. step (over)
6. raining
7. be
8. slip
9. fall (down)
10. get (up) (out)
11. look (at)
12. go (back)
13. stamp
14. jump
15. change

A BEAUTIFUL DAY (p. 104)

1. what
2. sigh
3. go
4. stretch
5. yawn
6. lie (down)
7. is (it's) (there's)
8. are (you're)
9. sweating
10. sit (up) (down)
11. look (for)
12. walk (over)
13. sleep

IT'S RAINING (p. 105)

1. are (you're)
2. walking, walk
3. start (to)
4. raining
5. take (out) (off)
6. open
7. stop
8. shake (off)
9. close
10. hurry

A WINDY DAY (p. 106)

1. is (it's)
2. are (you're)
3. walking
4. blowing
5. zip (up)
6. lean
7. come
8. chase
9. grab
10. give (back)
11. go (on)

A SNOWY DAY (p. 107)

1. is (it's)
2. look
3. snowing
4. go
5. put (on)
6. walk

A FOGGY DAY (p. 108)

1. are (you're)
2. driving, drive
3. is (it's)
4. see (can't) (can)
5. going
6. turn (on)
7. slow (down)
8. hunch (over)
9. watch (for)
10. lifting

A SUNNY DAY (p. 109)

1. shining
2. take
3. get (into) (up)
4. go (out) (into)
5. spread
6. rub
7. turn (on) (over)
8. find
9. lie (down)
10. close
11. fall (don't)
12. is (it's)
13. sweating
14. fill
15. spray
16. smile
17. feel

Prepositions

A Lost Umbrella

Directions: Write sentences to describe the action in the pictures.

Look	on in under on top of behind	the	closet table bookcase sofa newspapers chair

1. _____

2. _____

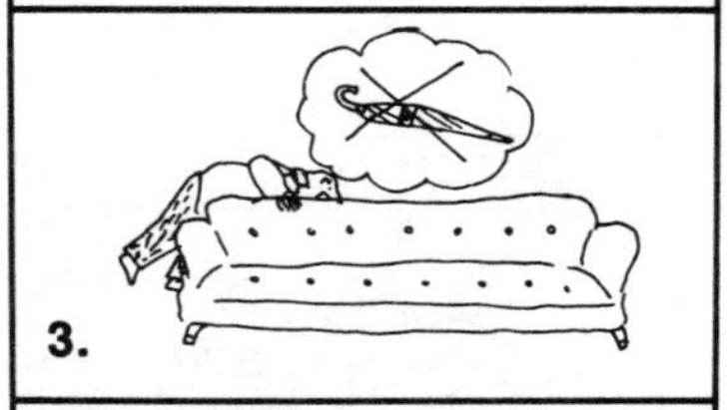

3. _____

4. _____

5. _____

6. _____

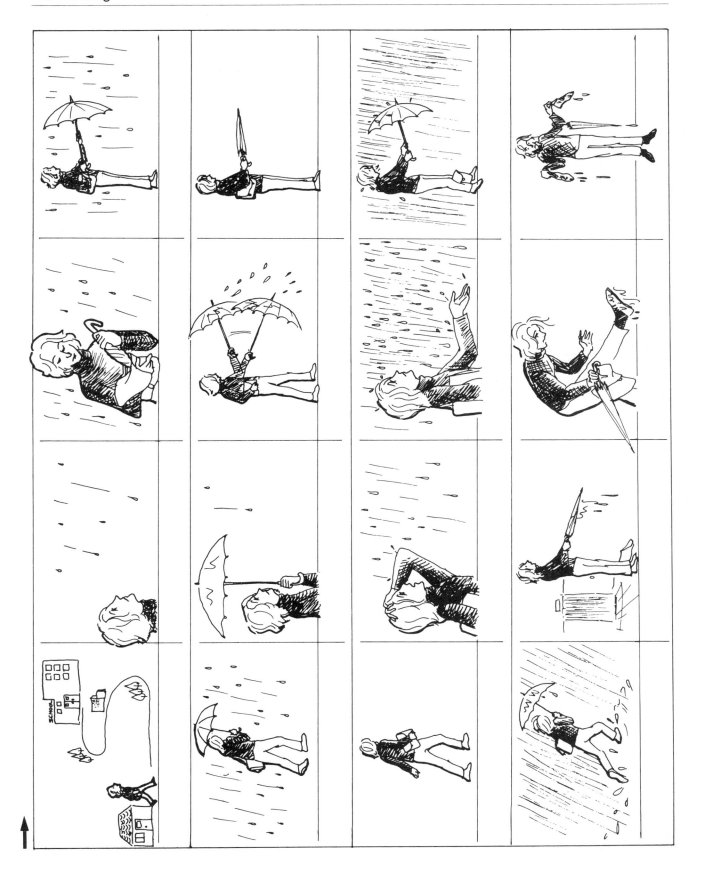

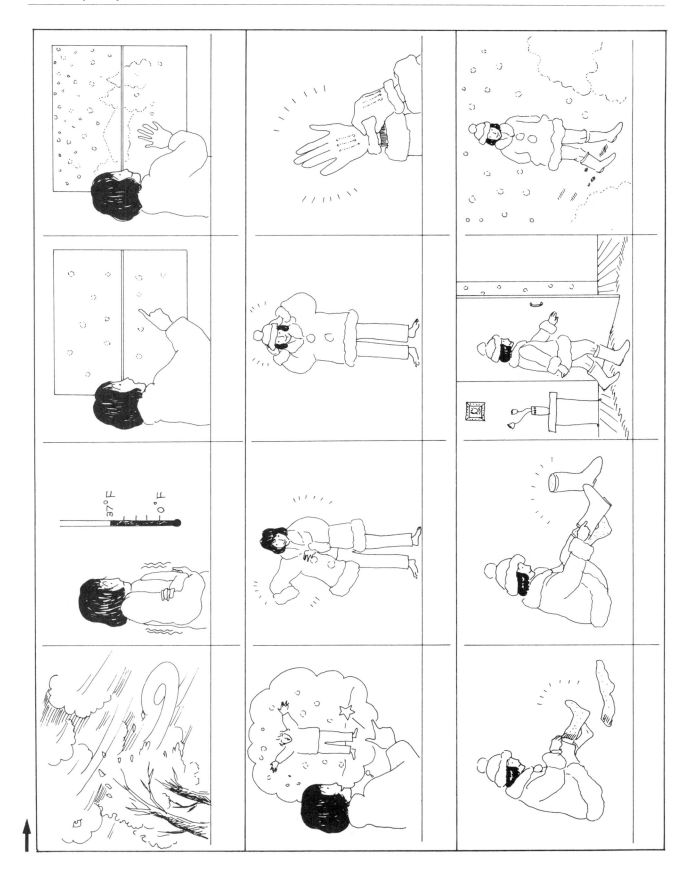

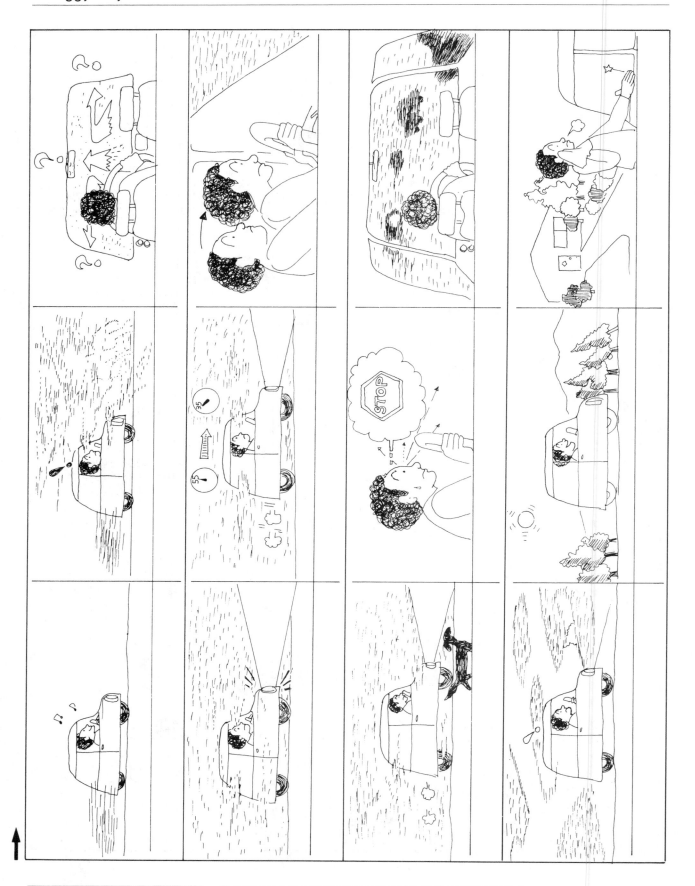

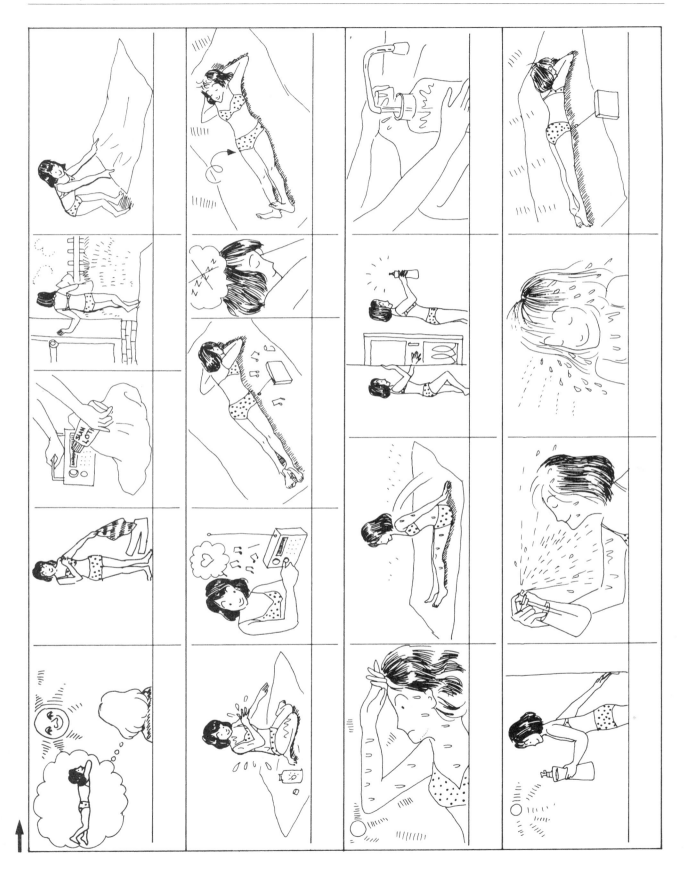

References

The books listed below contain background information related to *ACTION ENGLISH PICTURES* and/or additional lesson material for the indicated units in parentheses.

Asher, James J. *Learning Another Language Through Actions: The Complete Teacher's Guidebook.* Los Gatos, Calif.: Sky Oaks Productions, 1977.

Carver, Tina, and Fotinos, Sandra D. *A Conversation Book: English in Everyday Life.* Englewood Cliffs, N.J.: Prentice-Hall, Inc., 1977.

Fein, Elizabeth. *Speak for Yourself, Book 1.* Rowley, Mass.: Newbury House, 1984.

Ferreira, Linda. *Notion by Notion.* Rowley, Mass.: Newbury House, 1981. **(Units 4, 7)**

Graham, Carolyn. *The Electric Elephant and Other Stories.* Oxford: Oxford University Press, 1982. **(Unit 4)**

_____. *Jazz Chants.* Oxford: Oxford University Press, 1978. **(Units 1, 2, 7)**

Hartley, Bernard, and Viney, Peter. *American Streamline Departures.* Oxford: Oxford University Press, 1983. **(Units 4, 7)**

Keyes, Joan R. *Beats! Conversation in Rhythm for English as a Second Language.* Freeport, N.Y.: Educational Activities, Inc., 1983.

Molinsky, Steven J., and Bliss, Bill. *Side by Side, Books 1 and 2.* Englewood Cliffs, N.J.: Prentice Hall Regents, 1980. **(Units 1, 2, 4, 7)**

Olsen, Judy W-B. *Look Again Pictures.* San Francisco, Calif.: Alta Book Center Publishers, 1998 (Alemany Press, 1984).

Romijn, Elizabeth, and Seely, Contee. *Live Action English.* Berkeley, Calif.: Command Performance Language Institute, 1997.

Segal, Bertha E. *Teaching English Through Actions* (French, Spanish, German, English editions). Brea, Calif.: Berty Segal, Inc., 1981.

Weinstein, Nina J. *Communication Skits.* Englewood Cliffs, N.J.: Prentice Hall Regents, 1983.

Yorkey, Richard C. *Talk-a-Tivities: Problem Solving and Puzzles for Pairs.* Menlo Park, Calif.: Addison-Wesley Longman Publishing Co., 1985.

APPENDIX 1: Picture Sequences Text

UNIT 1 TEXT   GOING TO BED (p. 6)

1. It's 10 PM. You're watching TV.
2. The program is finished.
3. You're very tired.
4. Get up and turn off the TV.
5. Stretch and yawn.
6. Go to your bedroom.
7. Turn on the lights.
8. Sit on the bed and take off your shoes and socks.
9. Stand up and get undressed.
10. Take off your sweater. Take off your pants.
11. Put on your pajamas.
12. Pull back the covers on your bed.
13. Turn off the lights.
14. Get into bed.
15. Put your head on the pillow.
16. Pull up the covers and . . .
17. Go to sleep.
18. Dream about your family.

MAKING TEA (p. 15)

1. You want some tea.
2. Go to the kitchen.
3. Get the teapot.
4. Fill the pot with water.
5. Put the teapot on the stove.
6. Turn the dial to hot.
7. The water is boiling.
8. Turn the dial to off.
9. Take a tea bag.
10. Put the tea bag in a cup.
11. Pour hot water in the cup.
12. The tea is very hot.
13. Put some milk in the tea.
14. Drink some of the tea.
15. Give a cup of tea to your friend.
16. The tea is fantastic!

UNIT 2 TEXT   AT THE DOCTOR'S OFFICE (p. 22)

1. You're at the doctor's office.
2. You don't feel well.
3. The doctor comes in.
4. She shakes your hand.
5. She asks, "What's the matter?"
6. You tell her, "I have a headache. I have a backache. I have the chills."
7. She takes your temperature.
8. She takes your pulse.
9. She listens to your heart.
10. She looks at your eyes.
11. She looks in your ears.
12. She says, "Open your mouth and say ahhhhh."
13. She looks at your tongue and your throat.
14. She tells you, "I think you have the flu. Go home and go to bed."

A DENTAL APPOINTMENT (p. 27)

1. You are sitting in the dentist's reception room.
2. You have a terrible toothache.
3. Press your hand to your cheek.
4. Say, "OHHHHH, my tooth hurts."
5. Look at your watch.
6. Call out, "OHHHH my tooth hurts."*
7. The receptionist finally calls your name.
8. Follow her into the examining room.
9. Sit down in the dentist's chair.
10. The dentist comes in.
11. He asks, "What's the problem?"
12. Tell him, "I have a toothache."
13. Open your mouth wide.
14. He can't see. Open your mouth wider.
15. He examines your tooth.
16. It hurts. Clench your fists.
17. He says you need a filling.
18. Think about other things while he fills your tooth.

*Other options:
"This pain is killing me!"
"I can't stand it!"

FIRE! (p. 31)

1. You're preparing dinner. Your baby* is playing on the floor.
2. Oh! The frying pan is on fire.
3. Quick, put a cover on the pan.
4. Uh oh, the fire's too big. It's all over the stove.
5. Grab your baby* and leave the kitchen.
6. Close the kitchen door behind you.
7. Pick up the telephone and dial 911.
8. Tell the operator, "There's a fire in my kitchen."
9. Give the operator your name and address.
10. Yell, "Fire!" and tell everyone to get outside.
11. Close all the doors and run outside.
12. Whew! Here comes the fire department.
13. They certainly are fast.
14 Comfort your crying children.*
15. Thank goodness! The fire is out. It wasn't too bad.

*Substitute: grandchild, grandbaby, little baby, the baby, etc.

UNIT 3 TEXT WASHING DISHES (p. 45)

1. You need to wash the dishes.
2. Fill the sink with hot water.
3. Squeeze in some detergent.
4. Rinse the food off the plates.
5. Put the dishes in the soapy water.
6. Scrub the dishes.
7. Rinse the dishes with hot water.
8. Put the dishes in the rack.
9. Let the water out of the sink.
10. Sprinkle cleanser in the sink.
11. Scrub the sink.
12. Rinse the sink.

DUSTING (p. 46)

1. Get a soft cloth.
2. Go into the living room.
3. Dust the top shelf.
4. Dust the middle shelf.
5. Dust the bottom shelf.
6. Dust the table and the lamp next to the sofa.
7. Clean the dead bugs off the window sill.
8. Put the cloth on the end of the broom.
9. Get rid of the cobwebs in the corners with your broom.
10. Plug in the vacuum cleaner.
11. Vacuum the living room.
12. Now it's clean. It looks good.

UNIT 4 TEXT EATING OUT (p. 56)

1. You and your friend want to eat out.
2. Decide what kind of food you want. Chinese? Italian? American?
3. Go into the restaurant.
4. Follow the host/hostess to a table.
5. Sit down and look over the menu.
6. The waiter/waitress* asks, "Are you ready to order?"
7. Order some chicken, a small green salad, and french fries.
8. Your friend orders fish and rice.
9. The waiter/waitress* brings your dinner.
10. Eat your dinner. It's delicious.
11. The bus boy clears the dirty dishes.
12. The waiter/waitress asks, "Would you like anything else?"
13. Order some coffee and dessert.
14. S/he brings your check with your dessert and coffee.
15. Finish your coffee and dessert.
16. Pay for your dinner.
17. Don't forget to leave a tip for the waiter/waitress.

* Substitute: server (for a gender-free title).

THE POST OFFICE (p. 60)

1. You're at the post office.
2. You're going to mail a package to a friend.
3. Wait in line.
4. Smile at the person in front of you.
5. Smile at the person in back of you.
6. The line is moving.
7. It is your turn next.
8. Take your package to the counter.
9. Give it to the clerk.
10. Tell him you want to send it third class.
11. The clerk weighs the package.
12. He checks the cost for a third class package.
13. He tells you how much it costs.
14. Give the clerk the money.
15. He says, "Thank you."
16. Tell him, "You're welcome," and leave the post office.

UNIT 5 TEXT CHRISTMAS (p. 74)

1. It's Christmas time.
2. Wrap gifts for your friends and family.
3. Sing Christmas carols.
4. Put a wreath on the door.
5. Bake Christmas cookies.
6. On Christmas Eve, write a letter to Santa Claus.
7. Hang up your stockings.
8. Leave milk and cookies for Santa.
9. Put the childrren to bed. Tuck them in.
10. Put presents under the Christmas tree.
11. On Christmas morning, wake up early.
12. Surprise! Pick up the gifts and shake them.
13. Unwrap your presents.
14. Play with your new toys.
15. Have a big Christmas dinner with your friends and family.
16. Say, "Merry Christmas!"

VALENTINE'S DAY (p. 75)

1. It's February 14th. It's Valentine's Day.
2. You want to give Valentines to your friends.
3. Get some red (pink) paper.
4. Fold it in half.
5. With a pencil, draw half a heart on your paper next to the fold.
6. Get some scissors.
7. Cut along the line.
8. Unfold the heart.
9. Write "Happy Valentine's Day" in the middle of the Valentine card.
10. Give the Valentine to a special person. (friend, mother, father, etc.)
11. Also give your friend some flowers and candies and a kiss.
12. Say, "Happy Valentine's Day!"

A SUNDAY DRIVE (p. 77)

1. It's Sunday and you are going for a ride to the country.
2. Start your car.
3. Look in front of you and behind you.
4. Pull out into the moving traffic.
5. Drive with the traffic.
6. Slow down for the stop signal.
7. Signal for a right turn.
8. Turn on the green light.
9. You drive through a tunnel.
10. Your children* count the cars going by.
11. You drive over a bridge.
12. Look at the trees. You're out in the country.
13. Your children* are hungry and want to stop.
14. Stop your car, get out and stretch.
15. Look for a place for a picnic.
16. Spread out your blanket and take a nap.

* Substitute: grandchildren, the children, etc.

AT THE BEACH (p. 79)

1. It's a hot day. You're at the beach.
2. Unfold your beach chair and sit down.
3. Put on your sunglasses and sunhat.
4. Look at all the people at the beach.
5. Stare at the good-looking people.
6. Watch the children playing in the sand.
7. Smile at everyone.
8. It's hot. You're sweating.
9. Stand up. Look at the ocean.
10. Take off your sunglasses and sunhat. You can cool off in the water.
11. Run into the water.
12. Oh, it's cold. Jump up and down.
13. Here comes a wave. Run back towards the beach.
14. Run into the water again.
15. Here comes another wave. Run towards the wave and dive in.
15. The water is fantastic. Swim around and have a good time.

UNIT 6 TEXT DOING HOMEWORK (p. 86)

1. You have a lot of homework today.
2. Get your books, paper, and pencil ready.
3. Sit down to study.
4. Open your book.
5. You're hungry. Go get an apple.
6. Go back to your homework.
7. Your favorite TV program is on.
8. Go watch TV.
9. The program is over.
10. Go back to your homework.
11. You want to listen to music.
12. Turn on the radio. (stereo)
13. The music is great! Dance around.
14. It's getting late. You have to get to work.
15. Sit down and do your homework.
16. Finally, you're finished.
17. Put all your stuff away.

GETTING READY FOR A TEST (p. 89)

1. You have a test tomorrow. You have to study.
2. Get all your notes and books together.
3. Sit down at your desk.
4. Open your notebook.
5. Read your notes.
6. Close your eyes and repeat what you've read.
7. Check your notes. Good, you remembered.
8. Underline some important words.
9. Think about what you've learned.
10. Ask your brother (sister) to ask you some questions.
11. Oh, this is hard. Look worried.
12. Answer the questions.
13. Good, you know the answers. Relax.
14. You need rest. It's time to go to bed.
15. Get your books together for tomorrow.
16. Go to bed.
17. Dream about passing the test.

TAKING A TEST (p. 90)

1. You have a test at school today.
2. You're very nervous.
3. Look at your notes.
4. Your teacher is ready to start.
5. Take one last peek.
6. Put your books away.
7. Here is your test paper.
8. Oh, this is terrible.
9. You can't remember anything.
10. You're sweating.
11. Tell yourself to relax.
12. Take a deep breath.
13. Exhale.
14. Look at your test again.
15. Good, you know the first answer.
16. Go ahead and answer the other questions.
17. This test isn't so hard after all.

SICK AT SCHOOL (p. 91)

1. You're sitting in class.
2. You don't feel well.
3. Put your head in your hand.
4. Your teacher asks, "Are you OK?"
5. Tell him/her, "I don't feel well."
6. S/he writes a note to the school nurse.
7. Take the note to the nurse.
8. Give the note to the nurse
9. The nurse asks, "What's the matter?"
10. Say, "I feel sick. My head aches. I have the chills."
11. She takes your temperature.
12. It's 100 degrees. You have a fever.
13. The office clerk calls your home.
14. Someone in your family comes to pick you up.
15. Go home.
16. Go to bed.

LATE TO CLASS (p. 92)

1. You're late.
2. Hurry to school.
3. Drop your books.
4. Pick them up quickly.
5. Hurry! Faster! You're really late.
6. Stop at the clasroom door.
7. Open the door very quietly.
8. All the students are listening to the teacher.
9. Tiptoe into the classroom.
10. Everyone turns and looks at you.
11. Blush. You're embarrassed.
12. Drop your books again.
13. Say, "Sorry I'm late teacher" and pick up the books.
14. Your teacher smiles patiently.
15. Sit down quickly.
16. Coming in late is embarrassing.

TAKING A BREAK (p. 93)

1. You're in class.
2. It's time for a break.
3. Get up and stretch.
4. Leave your pencil and books on the desk.
5. Go out of the classroom.
6. Lean against the wall.
7. Talk to your classmates.
8. You're hungry; you want a snack.
9. Get something from the vending machine.
10. Sit down and eat your snack.
11. Laugh and joke with your friends.
12. Look at your watch. Break is over.
13. Hurry back to your class.
14. Good. You made it just in time.

GOING TO THE LIBRARY (p. 94)

1. You're going to return some books.
2. Go to the library.
3. Take your books to the return desk.
4. The librarian checks your books.
5. Uh oh, one is overdue.
6. You have to pay a fine.
7. Now look at some books on the shelves.
8. You like mystery and biography.
9. Choose one mystery and one biography.
10. You also want some books about China (Mexico, Egypt . . .)
11. Ask the librarian where to find them.
12. Pick out a few books and take them over to a table.
13. Look them over. They look very interesting. You want to check them out.
14. Take your books to the check-out desk.
15. Show your library card to the clerk. Let him/her check out your books.
16. Say thank you and take your books home.

1. You're walking to school.
2. It starts to rain.
3. Take out your umbrella.
4. Open the umbrella.
5. Walk in the rain.
6. The rain is stopping.

7. Shake the water off your umbrella.
8. Close the umbrella.
9. Continue walking to school.
10. Oh dear, it's starting to rain again.
11. It's raining very hard.

12. Quickly open your umbrella.
13. Hurry through the rain.
14. You made it. Close your umbrella.
15. Oh, oh, your feet are completely wet.
16. Take off your wet shoes.

A WINDY DAY (p. 106)

1. It's a windy day.
2. You're walking down the street.
3. The leaves are blowing in the wind.

4. Zip up your jacket.
5. Lean into the wind.
6. Here comes a man's hat.
7. Chase it.

8. Grab it.
9. Give it back to the man.
10. Go on your way.

A SNOWY DAY (p. 107)

1. It's a winter day.
2. It's getting cold.
3. Look! It's beginning to snow.
4. It's snowing harder.

5. You want to go out in the snow.
6. Put on a warm coat.
7. Put on a snow hat.
8. Put on warm gloves.

9. Put on wool socks.
10. Put on your boots.
11. You're ready. Go outside.
12. Take a walk in the falling snow.

A FOGGY DAY (p. 108)

1. You're driving down the street.
2. Oh! It's foggy.
3. You can't see where you're going.
4. Turn on your headlights.

5. Slow down.
6. Hunch over the steering wheel.
7. Drive slowly down the street.
8. Watch for the stop signs.
9. Watch for the other cars.

10. The fog is lifting.
11. Oh good, you can see now.
12. You're home. What a relief.

A SUNNY DAY (p. 109)

1. The sun is shining brightly. You're going to sunbathe.
2. Get into your bathing suit.
3. Get your towel, suntan lotion, and radio.
4. Go out to your backyard.
5. Spread out your towel.
6. Rub suntan lotion with sunscreen all over yourself.

7. Turn on the radio. Find your favorite music station.
8. Lie down on your stomach.
9. Close your eyes. Don't fall asleep.
10. It's hot. Turn over on your back.
11. It's very hot. You're sweating.
12. Get up.

13. Go into your house and get a spray bottle.
14. Fill the bottle with cold water.
15. Take the bottle outside.
16. Spray yourself with water.
17. Ahhhhh. Smile. That feels good.
18. Lie down in the sun again.

Picture Sequences Text

Following are the picture sequences in *ACTION ENGLISH PICTURES* which have accompanying text in *LIVE ACTION ENGLISH*.

<table>
<tr><td>*Action English Pictures*
sequence page number</td><td>*Live Action English*
page number</td></tr>
</table>

Unit 5 Holidays and Leisure

Unit 6 At School

Unit 7 Weather